Global Democrat

Global Democratic Theory

A Critical Introduction

Daniel Bray
&
Steven Slaughter

polity

First published in 2015 by Polity Press

Polity Press
65 Bridge Street
Cambridge CB2 1UR, UK

Polity Press
350 Main Street
Malden, MA 02148, USA

ISBN-13: 978-0-7456-8087-3 (hardback)
ISBN-13: 978-0-7456-8088-0 (paperback)

A catalogue record for this book is available from the British Library.

Library of Congress Cataloging-in-Publication Data

Bray, Daniel, 1976–
    Global democratic theory: a critical introduction / Daniel Bray, Steven Slaughter.
       pages cm
    Includes bibliographical references and index.
    ISBN 978-0-7456-8087-3 (hardback : alk. paper) -- ISBN 978-0-7456-8088-0 (pbk. : alk. paper) 1. Democracy--Philosophy. 2. Globalization--Political aspects. I. Slaughter, Steven, 1970– II. Title.
    JC423.B767 2015
    321.8--dc23
                                    2014036703

Typeset in 10.5/12 Plantin by
Servis Filmsetting Limited, Stockport, Cheshire
Printed and bound in the United Kingdom by Clays Ltd, St Ives PLC

The publisher has used its best endeavours to ensure that the URLs for external websites referred to in this book are correct and active at the time of going to press. However, the publisher has no responsibility for the websites and can make no guarantee that a site will remain live or that the content is or will remain appropriate.

Every effort has been made to trace all copyright holders, but if any have been inadvertently overlooked the publisher will be pleased to include any necessary credits in any subsequent reprint or edition.

For further information on Polity, visit our website:
politybooks.com

Contents

Acknowledgments

This book emerged from a joint belief that our various reflections on the problems and future possibilities of democracy were occurring within a distinct subset of broader accounts of democratic and political theory. These reflections are expressed in a literature that examines the changing nature of democratic theory and practice in a context of globalization, global governance, and transnational civil society. We refer to this literature as "global democratic theory" and believe that it can play an important role in guiding contemporary movements for democratization. As such, the primary aim of the book is to provide academics, students, and politically engaged citizens with an accessible account of the impact of globalization on democracy, the main theories of global and transnational democracy that have been developed in response, and a critical analysis of their key claims and prospects in practice. We hope the book will be a significant contribution to the literature because there is currently no single volume that brings together the scholarship of global democratic theory in this time of increased attention to globalization and democratic change. Given that so many scholars working in this area have published in Polity Press over the last two decades, it seemed appropriate to publish this book with them, so our first thanks go to the many staff at Polity who have supported this area of scholarship over the years. A special thank you also goes to the people who specifically contributed to the production of this book, particularly Louise Knight for her initial interest in the project.

This project was made possible with the help of a number of people who contributed invaluable academic and personal support. Steven would like to thank Andrew Scott and the School of Humanities and Social Sciences at Deakin University for their assistance and support.

We would also like to thank several research assistants who helped in various stages of this project, including Uschi Steedman and Mark Ryan. On a personal note, Steven would like to thank Yvette, Zara, and Lucinda for their love and support during the writing of this book. Its final stages coincided with the birth of Lucas Nakata Bray who has brought boundless joy and many sleepless nights to Daniel's life over the past year. A very special thank you goes to Sana for her love, patience, and strength during this time.

Introduction:
Democratic Theory in a Global Era

The contemporary global era is characterized by new modes of power and authority as well as shifting patterns of social interaction in which democratic ideas have an uncertain place. This uncertainty stems from the fact that democracy has become the main principle of legitimate political rule at the same time as global forces outside democratic control have increased in importance and threaten established forms of public representation, participation, and accountability located within the state. To varying degrees, democratic relationships of representation and accountability between citizens and their state are increasingly blurred as political decision-making becomes more densely embedded within complex and overlapping forms of globalization and global governance. Indeed, the contemporary era is characterized by the increased significance of global and transnational forms of authority comprised of regional and International Governmental Organizations (IGOs) like the European Union (EU) and the United Nations (UN), and networks of civil society actors ranging from networks of activists such as the World Social Forum (WSF), to networks of experts such as international science academies and the World Economic Forum (WEF). Furthermore, the power of the state to organize economic life is now significantly conditioned by the operation of global market forces and transnational corporations (TNCs). Generally speaking, there has been a displacement of decision-making from the state to global forms of governance and global markets. In this context, David Held (1998: 21) claims that "the idea of a political community of fate – of a self-determining collectivity which forms its own agenda and life conditions – can no longer meaningfully be located within the boundaries of a single nation-state alone."

These global and transnational dynamics have created a number of significant challenges to contemporary understandings of democracy. First, the core democratic capacities of states are undermined by the growing ability of global governance and global markets to limit the meaningful choices available to governments and their people. Second, the shift of power to global and regional institutions creates "democratic deficits" where increasingly numerous and complicated tasks of policy-making are conducted beyond the accountability and oversight of the domestic publics of democratic states. Third, new political opportunities for promoting democratic practices have arisen in global and transnational networks involving a host of NGOs, social movements, and experts (Scholte 2002, 2011b; Dryzek 2011). On many issues, for example, human rights activists, business elites, refugees, climate change scientists, and religious leaders claim to speak for global or transnational constituencies that go beyond state interests. Many of these actors claim to serve democratic functions of representation or public scrutiny, or make demands for more inclusion and accountability in global governance in the name of democracy. Overall, the impact of globalization on democracy appears considerable and the

> implications of this are troubling, not only for the categories of consent and legitimacy but for all the key ideas of democracy: the nature of a constituency, the meaning of representation, the proper form and scope of political participation, the extent of deliberation, and the relevance of the democratic nation-state as the guarantor of the rights, duties and welfare of subjects. (Held 2006a: 292)

In this context, traditional understandings of democracy are under significant challenge, prompting the development of new theories and practices that attempt to grapple with these transformations and create democratic mechanisms that transcend the nation-state.

This book examines how democratic theory has sought to engage with these changing contours of democracy in light of the impacts of globalization and global governance. Democratic theory is the field of scholarship that examines the challenges and possibilities of public rule and in recent decades has increasingly considered the ways in which the democratic practices of the state are being undermined by contemporary global forces. Indeed, Anthony McGrew (2002b: 269) points to a "transnational turn" in democratic theory: a widespread contention that democracy needs to be rethought in light of the impact of globalization. Many scholars are exploring how democracy can adapt to a globalizing world by examining prospects for democratic institutions beyond the state, as well as developing the democratic potential of transnational activism, civil society, and global public spheres (Archibugi and Held 2011; Bohman 2007; Bray 2011; Dryzek 2006; Goodin 2010; Scholte 2011b). At the heart of this literature are a variety of different normative proposals for democratic change in response to the impact of globalization. These proposals critically examine whether the state needs to be transformed in order to be democratic in this context, and challenge long-held assumptions that democracy must reside within the state by developing arguments for democracy at the global or transnational level. This book critically analyzes these proposals to identify the problems and possibilities of global and transnational democracy.

The central premise of this book is that the possibilities of democracy are being reshaped by globalization and global governance in ways that provide both new obstacles and opportunities for democratic practice. This has generated significant scholarly and public debates about the prospects of democracy in a global era. This book refers to this literature as "global democratic theory" and provides an assessment of the value of this scholarship and the possibilities associated with rethinking and redesigning the practice of democracy, including the possibility of creating democracy beyond the state. In order to provide a systematic examination of how specific accounts of democratic theory have responded to globalization, this book considers three key questions:

(1) What are the problems that accounts of global democratic theory seek to address?
(2) What are the normative claims of different accounts of global democratic theory?
(3) To what extent are these accounts of democratic theory feasible?

These questions guide our examination of the various proposals for altering the substance and scope of democracy, including developing democratic practices beyond the nation-state. The one thing that is relatively certain is that anything we might one day call democracy beyond the state will not look the same as the democracy within the state (Dryzek 2011: 214). Indeed, the approaches considered in this book reveal a wide range of views about the future of democracy and its possible extension to the global level. By examining the development of global democratic theory, this book provides glimpses of what these democratic futures might be.

Globalization and Democratic Theory

Global democratic theory has attempted to rethink democracy by considering the impacts of globalization. While the meaning of democracy is fundamentally contested, the underlying idea that most scholars share is that democracy entails the political practices through which the people govern themselves, which contrasts with oligarchy and dictatorship. While democracy has its origins in the direct rule of an assembly of citizens in ancient city states, since the eighteenth century the idea of democracy has become associated with public rule within a nation-state. Modern democracy is institutionalized as a representative system that involves competitive elections and a publicly determined rule of law which "came to be practiced (and only practicable) in a territorial entity with definite borders wrapped around a people who constituted a nation" (Saward 2006: 402–3). The spread of representative democracy during the twentieth century precipitated an exponential growth in democratic theory scholarship addressing questions regarding the social preconditions for democracy, the ways democratic institutions could be more effective and accountable to the public, and, importantly for the purposes of this book, a core concern with how democracy can adapt to changing political contexts.

At its heart, democratic theory is the field of scholarship that examines the normative purpose and scope of democratic practice, the nature, scale, and membership of democratic communities, and the design of democratic institutions. In this literature, democracy does not just refer to electoral democracy; it refers more broadly to the various overlapping ways in which citizens interact and influence public decision-making processes. Indeed, democracy is an idea and political practice that has always been in flux. Democratic publics and the scholars studying them have always had to respond to changing social, economic and political developments. As Michael Saward (2001: 581) argues:

> The idea of "democracy" has always contained within it the seeds of its own transformation. Today, what we mean by the concept is rapidly in the process of becoming more diverse, less symmetrical, more malleable, more complex. In this sense, we may need to become relaxed about a new, "pick-and-mix" conception of procedural democracy. Various devices (such as elected legislatures, citizens' deliberative forums, the initiative and referendum) are in principle available to enact particular understandings of basic democratic principles of equality, freedom, inclusion, and so on, at different levels of political community. In the

light of these points, we can say that a more permissive approach to what may count as "democracy" may in turn foster (and endorse) a further period of fruitful and creative democratic design.

This acceptance of a permissive conception of democracy is important when we consider how the liberal democratic state might respond to globalization. For this purpose, it is important to keep a variety of democratic options on the table rather than focus on only one mechanism of democracy (such as elections) that might be inadequate on its own and forecloses opportunities to build new democratic innovations.

Democratic theory has overlapping analytical and normative aspirations which examine both the existence of *actual* forms of democratic practice as well as ethical or normative accounts of how democracy *ought* to be organized. John Dryzek (2004: 143–4) indicates that while liberal democracy has triumphed as the dominant model of democracy in political practice, there are a plethora of diverse and overlapping theories and proposals in democratic theory that contribute to debates about modern democracy and its future prospects. Some of these models are based on how existing political systems actually function; some focus on emerging or latent forms of public activity in which individuals engage with formal political systems like parliaments; and some are purely normative accounts of how democracy *should* operate. There is also a significant literature in broader political theory which grapples with issues of citizenship and civil society in liberal nation-states, the influence of civil society activity in global politics, as well as prospective theories of global citizenship and transnational civil society in alternative models that explore desirable pathways for democratic practice beyond the state. This work contains accounts of the relationship between a democratic public or *demos* and political authority, and also includes consideration of the appropriate scale of the *demos* and how such political communities should be created and preserved.

This scholarly focus is being stimulated by the widely shared recognition that emerging forms of globalization are challenging traditional forms of representation, participation, and accountability within states, as well as opening up new opportunities for political activity beyond the state. Globalization is understood in various ways by different theories of International Relations (IR) and political theory, but central to most understandings is the claim that globalization is a set of processes in which human activity in political, economic, and cultural domains is increasingly taking on a global dimension. As such, globalization has significant implications for the scope of politics and democracy. First, developments in communications technology have empowered a new range of actors to operate in politically significant ways (Held et al. 1999: ch. 1). While states remain important actors in global politics, clearly globalization has made it easier for NGOs, corporations, and terrorist groups to operate across territorial borders. Second, the practical interdependence and mutual reliance brought about by globalization is also being coupled with forms of moral interdependence involving forms of awareness that transcend national boundaries. Today, changing moral relationships are largely driven by increased recognition of global problems, including climate change and the human suffering associated with extreme poverty that plagues many parts of the world. Such recognition is due in part to increased media coverage – otherwise known as the "CNN effect" – and the work of NGOs and activists in publicizing these problems in the media and the Internet. Third, in many domains, the lines between foreign and domestic policy have blurred due to intense and widespread forms of global integration. Issues such as terrorism, nuclear proliferation, organized crime, and environmental protection that transcend national borders cannot be effectively tackled by individual states alone.

As a consequence, complex forms of cooperation have developed over recent decades that are generally referred to as "global governance". Global governance is a contested term but in essence refers to the various forms of international and transnational activity aimed at enabling cooperation on shared goals in the absence of an overarching political authority like a world government (Rosenau 1999; Barnett and Duvall 2005). Here, governance means forms of authority, cooperation or management – be they public or private, formal or informal – that lead to the coordination, control, or regulation of a social activity in order to achieve common goals. From this angle, the nation-state does not have a monopoly on governance and, while playing a central role, it is not the only political actor involved in exercising authority in the issue areas of security, economic prosperity, or environmental sustainability. It is now the case that organizations such as the UN, forums like the G20, regional bodies like the EU, and private organizations like TNCs, business councils, networks of experts and NGOs play an increasingly important role in policymaking (Hale and Held 2012). Jan Aart Scholte (2000: 138–9) argues that these public and private bodies are "supraterritorial constituencies" that are external influences over the operation of state policy-making. In these circumstances, the neat picture of political life contained within the nation-state is complicated by a complex web of governance networks that stretch across territorial borders, which are often highly technocratic and blur traditional lines of representation and accountability. Such networks often place power in the hands of political actors that are unelected and do not reside in the societies in which their decisions are implemented. These decisions may even override domestic regulation and run counter to local preferences, as they often do, for example, in relation to International Monetary Fund (IMF) loan conditionality. This means that global governance is often accused of undermining democracy within nation-states, driving calls for new avenues of participation and accountability for those excluded from networks of global authority.

In this context, some scholars also point to the increasing prominence of NGOs and transnational civil society in global politics as enabling new forms of democratic representation and public accountability, and leading to increasing forms of public engagement with global governance (Dryzek 2011, 2012). This is facilitated by developments in communications technology and the growing prevalence of transnational media networks. While the prospects for a formal electoral democracy at a global level are not strong, these forms of public engagement are democratic in the broader sense of attempting to moderate and hold authority to account that demonstrate some emerging potential for democratic practice beyond the state (Goodin 2010; Keane 2011). The growing numbers of NGOs, monitoring agencies, and global forms of media and communications have created political spaces beyond any one nation-state where state officials and representatives of IGOs often explain and give reasons for their decisions. In these spaces, citizens can engage or witness public discussion involving contests between competing arguments that informs their political views and choices. Recognizing emerging practices of transnational activism and civil society as potential signs of democratization does not imply an inevitable path toward global democracy, but it does widen our perspective beyond elections to see the possibilities for democracy in global governance.

Global Democratic Theory

Consequently, contemporary democratic theory engages in systematic reflection on the problems of existing forms of democratic practice within the state, as well as new possibilities offered by global governance and transnational civil society. This scholarship therefore opens up possibilities for forms of democracy which transcend the state. There are four key reasons why this type of scholarship is valuable, especially in response to contemporary globalization. First, a core focus of democratic theory is to examine the problems and controversies associated with existing forms of democratic practice. This involves forms of internal critique where a specific democratic practice is compared to its own guiding ideals, and also forms of external critique where a functioning democratic system is compared to the requirements of a prospective normative model of democracy. These critical inquiries can reveal gaps between what democracies claim they value and what they actually do, which can stimulate change and suggest conditions for improving the democratic quality of public life. Second, embedded in the vast majority of democratic theory is a deep respect for, and defence of, basic democratic values. While democratic values may be abridged or ignored in the cut and thrust of political life, democratic theory is a field of scholarship that affirms democratic values such as liberty, equality, accountability, civil society, and citizenship. Different scholars emphasize and interpret these values in often radically different ways, but there is underlying respect for democratic purposes and possibilities. In this way, democratic theory serves to remind citizens of the value of democracy and the reasons for adopting, safeguarding, and reforming it.

Third, there is considerable value in democratic theory's aim to develop ideal forms of democratic practice. If ideals articulate feasible transformations of existing practice, they can act as practical guides to the realization of normatively defensible forms of democracy and prompt public debates about how democracy could better meet public ends. However, even if these proposed models are not fully put into practice by citizens or policy-makers, they are still valuable as tools of criticism that can provide a contrast between an ideal form of democracy and political reality, and thereby expose the problems and biases of the status quo. Fourth, democratic theory focuses upon the ways that democracy can and should adapt to changing political conditions and societal expectations. As Saward indicated earlier, democracy always contains the "seeds of its own transformation." As an ongoing effort to oppose tyranny as well as meet public ends, democracy requires a constant evaluation of how this system of public rule can effectively attain these ends in light of changing political, economic, social and technological contexts. In this book, we explore how democratic theory has responded to the changes underway in the global era by analyzing the main approaches that seek to consider the democratic promise and problems of globalization.

This book examines global democratic theory as a distinctive body of scholarship by focusing upon five primary approaches to democracy under conditions of globalization. These approaches are: liberal internationalism, cosmopolitan democracy, transnational deliberative democracy, social democracy, and radical democracy. Liberal internationalist theory as argued by Robert Keohane, Anne-Marie Slaughter and others focuses upon a democratic ethic of reform where international institutions act on the cooperative priorities of states and are transparent and accountable to national governments in ways that support democracy at the level of the nation-state. The approach here is aimed at strengthening the existing legal structures of global governance and making IGOs more accountable to national governments. Cosmopolitan theorists like David Held, Daniele Archibugi, and Richard Falk, in contrast, argue for a democratic ethic of humanity which involves the creation of a democratic constitutional order for global governance based on social democratic values, human rights, and cosmopolitan law. Central to the long-term vision of cosmopolitans is the development of new overarching institutions like a global parliament and a major transformation of international relations that would undermine traditional practices of national sovereignty. Transnational deliberative democracy advances an ethic of dialogue as exemplified in the deliberative and republican scholarship of John Dryzek, James Bohman, and Philip Pettit. Unsatisfied with prevailing modes of liberal democracy, this ethic promotes an agenda that seeks to transform governance structures by enhancing the role of transnational deliberation and public reasoning in political life, even in IGOs not likely to be accountable via electoral processes. Transnational deliberation is possible through a range of non-electoral mechanisms like citizens' assemblies, deliberative polls, and deliberation within specific public spheres that can contest formal authority and incorporate affected people into decision-making processes.

The social democratic approach captures a diverse array of positions attempting to develop a democratic ethic of equality by regulating and possibly transforming global capitalism. This position encompasses efforts by scholars supportive of the Third Way, scholars such as Colin Crouch and Andrew Gamble, who seek to reform global capitalism, and more radical scholars such as Alex Callinicos who seek to promote a revolution that supplants capitalism. The core feature of this approach is the need to focus on the interests of workers and the politics of class in order to develop a state capable of regulating the global economy. Finally, the book considers the radical anarchist approach to democracy exemplified in the work of Michael Hardt and Antonio Negri. Their approach is grounded in an ethic of revolution that seeks to develop self-governing communities that can resist and overthrow the global system of sovereignty and capitalism. This radical approach argues that the democratic potential of "the multitude" can only be realized outside of the oppressions of "imperial sovereignty" and its corrupted system of property relations. Hardt and Negri envisage post-sovereign democracy grounded in a multiplicity of communities and social movements that challenge the constitutionalism and individualism of liberal politics and lead to a commonwealth that is constituted by new forms of cooperation and affection. However, they argue it is the constituent power of the people that makes democracy so its precise institutional forms cannot be detailed in advance.

This book adopts a practical approach that sees each of the approaches as a distinctive normative response to a core problem that globalization poses for democracy. This means the first task in analyzing each approach is to identify the problematic aspect of globalization that frames its core ethical purpose. Based on its particular reading of the problem, each approach suggests normative and practical solutions concerning the location of democratic authority, the nature of political community, and the institutional form of democracy in a context of globalization. This analysis is conducted by examining the most prominent scholars from each approach to outline its core features. As such, it does not claim to capture the entire range of views within each perspective, or indeed capture all forms of democratic or political theory. Furthermore, some scholars and their specific theories transcend any one of the approaches noted above. Scholars such as Dryzek, for example, demonstrate commitments to cosmopolitan and deliberative impulses. It is also the case that republican scholars can be placed within the liberal internationalist and deliberative positions (and possibly in the social democratic approach as well), feminist scholars can be found within each approach, and Green political theory appears within the deliberative and radical approaches. Consequently, as this book will make clear, the differences *within* these approaches are often just as important as the differences between them. We have also listed key readings at the end of each chapter to further emphasize the key authors and texts relevant to each chapter.

Importantly, the practical approach of this book allows a systematic examination of the prospects and possibilities for democratic change. By treating each approach as a normative resource directed at ameliorating the problematic aspects of globalization, an examination of its feasibility can be conducted based on an analysis of its proposed pathways of democratization and capacity to generate a constituency for change in a complex environment of complementary and opposing forces. Furthermore, this pragmatism also suggests that each approach need not be advocated or rejected as a whole; aspects of each approach can be used to shed light on different kinds of democratic deficits and as normative resources to promote democratic change in various contexts. Consequently, the underlying practical argument is that it is important see these various approaches as parts of an overarching body of theoretical work attempting to respond to contemporary globalization. Global democratic theory offers the greatest contribution when it articulates empirically relevant and normatively reasonable theories that can be used to guide democratic change in particular contexts, rather than by producing abstract models of global democracy that must be mechanically applied to the world as a whole.

Chapter Structure

This book examines and outlines global democratic theory in two parts. Part I explores the changes to practices of democracy and governance, which serves as the general empirical basis for constructing democratic responses to contemporary globalization. Chapter 1 examines the ways in which the changing role and uncertain future of the nation-state as a result of globalization presents significant challenges for prevailing notions of democracy within and beyond the state. The chapter first examines the different perspectives on the impact of globalization on the nation-state, outlining "hyperglobalist," "skeptical," and "transformationalist" explanations (Held et al. 1999: 3–8). It then considers some of the public reactions and debates about globalization, particularly with regard to the rise of neo-liberalism and the "hollowing out" of the state. Finally, the chapter discusses how democratic theory has reacted to these contemporary developments in its understandings of the role and significance of the state in democratic life. Chapter 2 examines contemporary global governance and its consequences for democracy by exploring the ways in which states and other actors create complex systems of rules and decision-making processes to address cross-border problems. It identifies the purposes and problems of contemporary global governance, including important concerns about the legitimacy of global rules and decision-making processes, and outlines the nature of transnational civil society and the possibilities of harnessing it to democratize global institutions. Finally, the chapter argues that the relationship between democracy and global governance has become an increasingly important issue for theorists in a rapidly expanding literature of global democratic theory.

Part II outlines and analyzes each of the five main approaches of global democratic theory in terms of its specific characterization of the problem of democracy, its particular normative claims, and the feasibility of its pathways of democratization. Chapter 3 focuses on liberal internationalism, which as indicated above aspires to make IGOs more accountable to national governments. In Chapter 4, we explore the cosmopolitan perspective that aspires to create a universal form of global democracy based on human rights and cosmopolitan law. Chapter 5 examines deliberative democracy and its concern with cultivating transnational public spheres in which there can be genuine dialogue between agencies of global governance and those affected by their policies. In Chapter 6, we analyze the social democratic response to globalization and its reformist and radical arguments for democratizing the capitalist basis of contemporary globalization. Finally, Chapter 7 outlines a radical anarchist approach to democracy that contests liberal and social democratic approaches wedded to capitalism and the state and instead argues for a post-sovereign world of self-governing communities on a global scale. Finally, the book concludes by considering the value of global democratic theory in helping citizens to rethink and redesign the organization of national and global governance. The conclusion also considers some of the pathways and design choices required to chart a more democratic future within a context animated by globalization and global governance.

Key Readings

Dryzek, J. (2004) Democratic political theory. In Gaus, G. and Kukathas, C. (eds.) *The Handbook of Political Theory*. Sage, London, pp. 143–54.

McGrew, A. (2002) Transnational democracy: theories and prospects. In Stokes, G. and Carter, A. (eds.) *Democratic Theory Today: Challenges for the 21st Century*. Polity, Cambridge, pp. 269–94.

Saward, M. (2001) Reconstructing democracy: current thinking and new directions. *Government and Opposition* 36 (4), 559–81.

Saward, M. (2006) Democracy and citizenship: expanding domains. In Dryzek, J., Honig, B., and Phillips, A. (eds.) *The Oxford Handbook of Political Theory*. Oxford University Press, Oxford, pp. 400–22.

1

Globalization and the Democratic State

A comprehensive examination of global democratic theory must begin with how globalization has impacted on the nation-state and the consequences for traditional conceptions of democracy. This is no easy task because the role of the state in the contemporary world is a contested issue within public debates and academic scholarship. The issue is further complicated by differences in how globalization is understood. For some scholars, globalization refers to a range of social processes that for many centuries have increased transnational and transcontinental interdependence, while for others globalization is conceived more narrowly as a process of economic integration involving the recent influence of neo-liberalism on the global economy. In either case, it is clear that the ideas and practices of neo-liberalism have ratcheted up the spatial process of global integration to unprecedented levels in recent decades (Steger 2009: 38–57). Today, people all over the world are involved in or affected by an array of global and transnational processes ranging from economic transactions on global financial markets to cultural exchanges on the Internet. However, it is also the case that the scope and impact of these practices are distinctly uneven: many people are excluded from sharing in the benefits of globalization, while others face serious burdens and disadvantages arising from their enmeshment in global networks of power. As a result, public reactions against contemporary globalization have been driven by the perception that there is little or no democratic control over new sites of power and authority that transcend the nation-state.

At the heart of these concerns are questions about what globalization means for the role and significance of the nation-state. Until the emergence of contemporary globalization, the state was assumed to be the primary reference point for understanding the nature of political community. Democratic theory largely assumed that the nation-state was central to democracy by defining "the people," their political rights, and framing what social purposes the people should pursue. The emergence of contemporary globalization has fundamentally challenged these assumptions. The changing role of the state presents considerable challenges to prevailing notions of political community and representative government that underpin democracy within the state. In order to explore these challenges, this chapter first explains the key features of a nation-state and then examines the different perspectives regarding the impact of globalization on state power and capabilities. It then considers the rise of neo-liberalism and some of the public reactions and debates about globalization in this context. Finally, the chapter examines how democratic theory has reacted to these developments in its understanding of the role of the state in contemporary democratic life.

The Modern State

In order to understand the changing role of the nation-state in contemporary global politics it is first necessary to define what a "state" is. The modern state is a historically specific type of polity that has spread across the world to become the predominate form of political organization. Due to the different historical trajectories in which they developed, states vary widely in their capabilities and in the type of political regime that controls them. States in the industrialized West and postcolonial Africa differ markedly in their ability to control their domestic economies, for example, and states might be further differentiated by liberal democratic, authoritarian, or theocratic systems of government. However, central to the development of all modern states is the notion of sovereignty manifest in control over a delimited territory and population. The modern state is a form of territorial rule that centralizes most of its key functions in a system of government that is backed by a monopoly over the legitimate use of force and the possession of the legitimate right of taxation. As Anthony Giddens (1985: 282) explains:

> a sovereign state is a political organization that has the capacity, within a delimited territory or territories, to make laws and effectively sanction their up-keep: exert a monopoly over the disposal of the means of violence; control basic policies relating to the internal political or admin-

istrative from of government; and dispose of the fruits of a national economy that are the basis of its revenue.

This capacity to rule involves an ability to create domestic law and enter into international legal arrangements, as well as playing a key role in shaping its population's identity and allegiance (Linklater 1998a: 118). By linking a vision of community to the administrative apparatus of the state, the "power over life and death" is legitimized by "appealing to and mobilizing deeper and more demanding feelings" of communal loyalty (Poggi 1978: 101).

The capacity for sovereign rule is also grounded in a state's right to supremacy in its domestic affairs and, by extension, a right to non-intervention by other states in its territory. Such rights are therefore conferred only by the recognition of sovereignty by other states and acknowledgment of the legal equality between them in an international society framed by shared rights, rules and responsibilities. This mutual recognition of sovereignty rose to prominence in the early modern period, as evident in the signing of the *Peace of Westphalia* that ended the Thirty Years War in Europe in 1648. In this period, European sovereigns began to recognize each other as equals and agreed not to interfere in each other's domestic affairs, particularly with respect to religious conflicts. In subsequent centuries, norms and practices of this so-called "Westphalian order" spread from Europe to the rest of the world and led to the development of international law, diplomatic communication, and other forms of cooperation between sovereign states. However, this expansion of the state system did not occur peacefully or without struggle. European countries violently imposed state structures on their colonial territories and did not recognize the sovereignty or existing political systems of the people they colonized. It was only when colonized people gained independence and sought to build their own states though a mixture of resistance and emulation that they gained sovereignty rights in the international system. Not all have been successful: many postcolonial states, particularly in sub-Saharan Africa, can be characterized as "weak" or "failed states" because they are unable to maintain domestic order and are prone to civil wars and humanitarian disasters that prompt external intervention, sometimes without the consent of the host government. Nevertheless, the processes of decolonization in the twentieth century marked the final decisive phase in which the state system became truly global.

While the sovereign state is an organization based on legal independence and collective administration, it also normally represents a political community that shares some basic ideas about its collective identity and how society ought to be governed. Since the early nineteenth century, nationalism has become the central ideology shaping the identity of political communities, and the associated quest for national self-determination has driven the proliferation of sovereign states. This is why contemporary states are referred to as "nation-states." Despite the prevalence of nationalism, however, its precise nature as an ideology and cultural practice is widely contested. Some scholars argue that the nation and nationalism rest on primordial conceptions of ancestry and territory, while others contend that nationalism is a modern phenomenon that has been constructed by political leaders in response to the breakdown of traditional societies (Gellner 1983). As a modern ideology, European nationalism developed in conjunction with and in response to the rise of popular sovereignty, the mobilization of mass armies, capitalism, and industrialism, and alongside the development of new forms of communication such as the printing press that generated a national consciousness in dispersed populations (Anderson 1991: 36). Ernest Gellner (1983: 1) argues that nationalism aims to unite the political sphere, understood as the state, with the cultural sphere, understood as the nation: "nationalism is primarily a political principle which holds that the political and the national unit should be congruent." This aspiration for political unity can lead to devastating consequences for territories where multiple nationalisms are present and the leaders of one nation use the state apparatus to oppress or eradicate the others, as was the case in the 1994 Rwandan genocide. Nationalism thus entails a special loyalty to members of one's nation that can ultimately supersede obligations to all other communities. As a moral ideal, this includes an ethic of public service and self-sacrifice that enables redistribution to fellow nationals through state welfare policies, and justifies the use of state violence in the defence of the nation against internal and external enemies.

However, in recent decades states have become embedded in global forms of governance addressing a range of global issues. Indeed, for much of the twentieth century states expanded their social and economic roles and developed international institutions dealing with a wide array of shared problems ranging from public health to ozone depletion. In this way, states play a crucial role in linking power to social and moral purposes both domestically and internationally (Eckersley 2004: 6; A. Slaughter 2004). States are thus Janus-faced in the sense that they look *inwards* to maintain order, administer public policy, and provide institutions for collective action, while also looking *outwards* to pursue the "national interest" by providing protection from external threats and cooperating with other state and non-state actors in order to address common problems. As such, states have played a key role beyond safeguarding their security by developing and implementing shared purposes like free trade, human rights and environmental protection that are intimately linked with processes of globalization. The relationship between the state and globalization is thus one of the key debates in contemporary political theory.

Perspectives on Globalization

The impact of globalization on state power has been a prominent issue in the globalization literature over recent decades with profound implications for how one thinks about politics. It is now uncontroversial to claim that globalization is a set of social processes where territorial borders are crossed on a regular basis by significant flows of people, resources, and ideas. However, the political implications of these flows and exactly what they mean for the nation-state and the future of governance is still debated. The seminal book *Global Transformations* (Held et al. 1999: 3–8) outlines three perspectives on globalization: the hyperglobalist; skeptical; and transformationalist positions. These broad positions do not fully capture the different views concerning the origin, scope, and causes of globalization, which can vary dramatically within each position, but they are useful reference points in understanding the consequences of globalization for the role and capabilities of the nation-state.

First, the *hyperglobalist* argument is that contemporary globalization is a new and revolutionary feature of global politics. Economic liberals who see globalization in terms of the extension of free trade and unfettered movements of money and investment tend to articulate this position. They contend that globalization is reshaping economic processes in ways that promote economic growth and material progress. In this context, hyperglobalists argue that the state is no longer able to shape economic priorities in its traditional functions of developing national economic policy or protecting national industries. That is, the nation-state has very limited capabilities because it is constrained by global market forces. Kenichi Ohmae (1995: 120), for example, claims that states are inadequate for a globalized economy, as they have become mechanisms of "wealth destruction" aimed at redistributing resources rather than engaging with mobile capital. Furthermore, hyperglobalists argue that many of the roles and functions of the nation-state are being transferred to global bodies such as the IMF and the World Bank. Nation-states are no longer sufficient in size or capability to be able to coordinate economic policy or to compete with private wealth, and instead such matters are increasingly falling within the domain of supranational or global authorities with the capacity to coordinate global policies. As Ohmae (1995: 11) puts it, nation-states are increasingly "nostalgic fictions" that have "*already* lost their role as meaningful units of participation in the global economy of today's borderless world."

In contrast, the *skeptical* argument questions whether globalization is particularly novel or is leading to the revolutionary changes that hyperglobalists identify. For the diverse range of scholars called "skeptics," the extent of globalization is dramatically overstated. Specifically, the claim that economic globalization is new and profoundly reshaping the world is a myth because in some respects the current *international* economy has only recently become as open and integrated as the regime in the *belle époque* between 1870 and 1914 (Hirst et al. 2009: 3). Furthermore, realists in the discipline of IR are skeptical of the existence of globalization because they argue that the world economy is still shaped by state-to-state interaction where strong states still exert their power to shape the international economy (Waltz 1999: 7). The key dynamic for realists is that states have different levels of power and capacity to influence or resist the drive of market forces and other forms of external influence. Marxists are also skeptical on the grounds that global interconnections have long been an essential part of the capitalist mode of production and hence nothing novel to the contemporary period (Harvey 1997: 421).

Not surprisingly, then, the skeptical approach argues against the notion that the state is powerless or obsolete. Linda Weiss (1998: 190), for example, in *The Myth of the Powerless State*, claims that hyperglobalists have tended "to overstate the past power of the state in order to claim state weakness in the present." She also argues that hyperglobalists have downplayed the diversity of state responses to competitive pressures. Weiss (1998: 190) points out that states around the world still make different strategic choices in their policies despite economic globalization. In general, skeptics of globalization contend that comparisons between countries around the world still demonstrate different economic and social policies in line with domestic values and preferences. As such, hyperglobalist accounts that exaggerate globalization are problematic (even dangerous) because they imply globalization is inevitable and ungovernable, and therefore any national reform strategies are paralysed in the face of global forces. If, however, the economic changes underway in the world today are more complex and equivocal than the hyperglobalists suggest, then the possibility remains that political action can be undertaken for the national and international control of markets in order to promote social goals (Hirst et al. 2009: 2). In this view, the state retains its crucial sovereign capacity to effectively legislate and implement public policy.

Third, the *transformationalist* perspective treats contemporary globalization as a multi-dimensional process that is reconfiguring the nature of political, social, and economic practice. As such, it seeks to tread a middle course between the hyperglobalists and skeptics and consequently has become the predominant position in this debate. The transformationalist position conceives globalization as a spatial process whereby various forms of human activity are increasingly traversing the globe and connecting people more densely and more quickly than ever before. Importantly, this position contends that globalization is not novel to the late twentieth century because global processes have been connecting individuals and polities for at least 500 years with some dynamics of globalization evident even earlier (like the spread of religions). However, the density and speed of these interconnections have accelerated in the late twentieth century due to advancements in technology that enable the formation of long distance social relationships. These relationships go beyond the economic realm as various global forms of social, cultural, and political activity increasingly connect people around the world. Globalization is fundamentally a spatial process evident in "the widening, deepening and speeding up of worldwide interconnectedness in all aspects of contemporary social life, from the cultural to the criminal, the financial to the spiritual" (Held et al. 1999: 2).

The transformationalist position on the impact of globalization on the capacities of the state emphasizes elements of both continuity and change. Where the hyperglobalists see globalization as bringing about the demise of the nation-state, and skeptics see the state as remaining supreme, transformationalists see globalization as reconfiguring or *transforming* the relationship between states, societies and markets (Held et al. 1999; Sørenson 2004). In this view, states continue to be important actors in global politics, but there have been significant changes in how states promote security and the welfare of their citizens in various policy fields. Indeed, there has been an internationalization of the state to such a degree that the very line between domestic policy and foreign policy is increasingly blurred in many areas (A. Slaughter 2004). For example, safeguarding public health now requires sophisticated international cooperation because increased flows of migrants, tourists, and businesspeople make it relatively easy to carry infectious diseases such as bird flu across national borders. Furthermore, transformationalists argue that TNCs, transnational social movements and international regulatory agencies have increased in power and significance in recent decades. As such, nation-states are no longer (if they ever were) the sole centres of power and authority or the principal forms of governance in the world today (Held and McGrew 2007: ch. 5). This is a significant shift in global politics: the state system is now one important part of a broader global system in which states must compete, cooperate, interact and generally coexist with a vast array of significant subnational, transnational and international actors that to a lesser or greater extent constrain state action (Rosenau 1992: 256).

The transformationalist position also highlights the shifts underway in notions of identity and allegiance embedded in the nation. Most transformationalists argue that modern political communities are historical and social constructions. Their particular form, coinciding with the territorial reach of the "imagined community," is a product of particular social and political conditions that led to the rise of nationalism in Europe and its spread throughout the globe (Anderson 1991). Today, however, singular forms of national identity are being undermined by changes in technology and communications, mass migration, and an awareness of a common human "fate." Andrew Linklater (1998b), for example, observes that political communities have always been in the process of reconstruction, and with intensifying globalization and regionalization, modern polities are experiencing significant transformations as new forms of post-national community emerge based around shared problems or social movements that transcend national politics. As such, national communities coexist today alongside "overlapping communities of fate" defined by the spatial reach of transnational networks, allegiances, and problems. Global problems like climate change, for example, demonstrate that the environmental future of one particular nation-state is connected to all others and these states interact with new transnational communities that bring together parliamentarians, bureaucrats, scientists, celebrities and citizens in a shared project to mitigate and adapt to global warming.

Neo-Liberal Globalization and the Competition State

Against the background of this debate, it is important to recognize that while contemporary forms of globalization are challenging the nation-state, it is not an idle bystander. Indeed, many scholars influenced by critical theory suggest that contemporary globalization is not natural or inevitable and is actively shaped by the policies of states. These scholars are keen to avoid the simplistic claims that the state remains unchanged in the face of globalization or that globalization represents a simple reduction of state power in the face of transnational flows (see Cerny 1995; Gill 1998, 2012; Held and McGrew 2007; Sassen 2003, 2006; Strange 1996). Rather, globalization is a set of processes driven by particular political ideas and interests. Consequently, this scholarship broadly accepts claims about increasing global integration, but points out that many scholars ignore the political forces that are championing the current form of economic globalization. In particular, "critical" scholars tend to emphasize the importance of neo-liberal ideologies and policies in shaping the global economy since the 1970s (Cox 1996; Gill 1998; Harvey 2005). Neo-liberal policies promoting free markets seek to open up national economies to global capital as well wind back the discretion of the state in economic life.

In this vein, Philip Cerny (2000, 2009) argues that contemporary states are becoming "competition states" which pursue policies quite different from post-war Keynesian projects of nation-building and the welfare state that sought to balance expanded international trade with redistribution within national societies. The development of the competition state represents a significant change in the relationship between states and markets. Instead of directly regulating or "taming" markets to serve social purposes, states support a free market order aimed at securing economic growth within national economies by establishing competitive advantages in the global economy. This means the international competitiveness of domestic industries is a key reference point for economic policy and the capacity of the state to attract capital becomes a primary focus of government. The focus on international competitiveness and the embrace of deregulation, liberalization, and privatization represents a significantly constrained role for the state in economic affairs that enables and entrenches a neo-liberal form of economic globalization. As such, Robert Cox (1996: 302) claims that the state has become "a transmission belt from the global to the national economy, where heretofore it had acted as the bulwark defending domestic welfare from external disturbances." The main implication is that states are becoming more responsive to global markets and international financial organizations than the interests and voices of large sections of their own population.

From this angle, we can see that although global processes transcend and circumvent the nation-state, globalization is still partially embedded in the territory of the states and dependent upon state policies for its particular trajectory. Saskia Sassen (2003: 242) uses the term "denationalization" to emphasize that globalization is not "something" that merely exists outside of the state, or between states, but is a political project that exists *inside* the policy framework of many states. The state is actively involved in granting rights to outside flows of people and resources, which leads to a "partial denationalizing of what had been constructed historically as national, including the exclusive territorial authority of the state." Far from being a bystander to globalization, states have undergone significant transformations as they negotiate new relationships between the national and the global:

> In the case of the global economy, this negotiation entails the development inside national states – through legislative acts, court rulings, executive orders, policy – of the mechanisms necessary for the reconstitution of certain components of national capital into "global capital," and necessary to develop and ensure new types of rights/entitlements for foreign capital in what are still national territories, in principle under the exclusive authority of their states. (Sassen 2003: 242)

Importantly, Sassen (2003: 243) argues that denationalization is not limited to economics because those states that engage with the international human rights regime, for example, can grant political and social rights to outsiders. Broadly speaking, however, less authority is delegated in policy-making areas relating to security or social policy, revealing that the prevailing dynamics of globalization are very much created by the political choices of governments with respect to domestic priorities and efforts to create international forms of cooperation.

Nevertheless, neo-liberal globalization presents the nation-state with some serious challenges, especially in light of the destabilizing impact of the 2008 global financial crisis (Gill 2012; Isakhan and Slaughter 2014). These challenges stem from a tension between the role of the state in safeguarding and representing a national community, and the imperative to create an economically flexible society that is competitive in global markets. That is, the competition state is faced with the difficult task of balancing national goals of distributive fairness, collective welfare and national solidarity, on the one hand, with global economic competitiveness, flexibility, and efficiency, on the other. In this context, the nation-state is in danger of losing its "legitimacy, institutionalized power and social embeddedness" as neo-liberal globalization compromises its capacity to enact policies that maintain social integration (Cerny 1997: 251). Despite the persistence of nationalism as a form of "social glue" across the world, it is argued that neo-liberal practices threaten the historical legitimacy of the nation-state in a number of significant ways.

First, the competition state is more constrained in the social policies it can readily enact. To the extent that states are shaped by neo-liberal financial orthodoxy and the operation of global markets, they have to consider both the reactions of these markets in formulating policy and withstand the consequences of financial bubbles and panics (Cerny 1997). In this context, there has been the "financialization" of global capitalism in the sense that financial markets have a growing structural influence relative to other forms of economic and political decision-making (Lapavitsas 2014). This financial discipline and the associated policies of austerity required to satisfy financial markets place serious limits on the ability of governments to pursue domestic policies that require large capital outlays in areas ranging from social welfare to infrastructure investments. Furthermore, the promotion of economic efficiency and competition usually requires labour market reform, liberalizing trade practices, and breaking up monopolies, including state enterprises. The state is thus "hollowed out" as its traditional functions of social provision are curtailed. Consequently, these reforms often clash with historically derived political or ethical principles based on the collective welfare of national communities. The practices of the competition state thus reflect tensions between competing goals of government that limit the domestic policy areas subject to democratic choice. To the extent that governments are seen to prioritize neo-liberal goals over domestic social welfare, the democratic notion that the state represents the interests and voices of national society is challenged.

Second, nation-states have become increasingly beholden to constituencies beyond their borders as a result of neo-liberal globalization. This can undermine the idea that the state is ultimately responsible to the society it represents. By choice or necessity, states sometimes prioritize the interests of global market actors over constituencies within the nation-state. For example, in the ongoing European economic crisis, governments have been forced to enact austerity measures as conditions for EU and IMF loans with little or no public consultation. In Heavily Indebted Poor Countries, the state is also often forced to cater to the interests of international creditors rather than the needs of domestic groups. In 2002, the UN Human Development Report documented that 29 African countries spent more on servicing the debt owed to foreign lenders than on health care (UNDP 2002: 209–10). Furthermore, almost all states seek to attract capital from foreign corporations to promote domestic investment and employment. These investments often provide great benefits to national economies, but they can also create relationships between states and corporations that benefit state officials and foreign shareholders but threaten the livelihoods of local people. Over recent decades, this has been evident in a number of mining and dam projects that have dispossessed or otherwise adversely affected local people, particularly indigenous communities. Because globalization has made the exit options for capital and corporations easier and more numerous, states are forced to placate foreign investors, sometimes to the detriment of the domestic constituencies that elected them.

Third, under the guidance of the competition state, the creation and implementation of government policy becomes enmeshed in the logic of the market. This is because government policy is not only locked into considering market reactions to economic and social policy, the state is also actively marketized in seeking to promote itself within global markets in a similar way to corporations (Cerny 1997: 251). This short-term, market-orientated approach to policy jeopardizes the ability of governments to pursue long-term democratic or social objectives. Specifically, the enactment of long-term social programs and public goods, such as those pursued by welfare states in many Western states during the twentieth century, become increasingly difficult and dependent on private capital within the constraints set by neo-liberal globalization. In order to reduce the costs of the state and avoid budget deficits, areas of public policy are "commodified" in the sense that they are at least partially cut loose from state intervention and become commodities subject to market forces. The privatization of health and education provision and the rise of public–private partnerships in infrastructure development throughout the world are key examples. In this way, the state actively extends market discipline into social and economic spheres previously quarantined from markets on the basis of the public interest or general welfare.

These changes threaten to undermine the historical legitimacy of the nation-state and its democratic justifications. The major implication of neo-liberalism and the financial orthodoxy of global capitalism is that governments find it difficult to uphold the protective and welfare functions crucial to this legitimacy. In one sense, the state is becoming an instrument, or a "transmission belt," built around the task of pursuing economic growth by liberalizing and deregulating social life and attracting global capital for domestic economic gain. This discipline can potentially clash with democratic responsibilities to the electorate and to long-term social objectives, risking the loss of the associative and public character that gives the state its legitimacy (Cerny 1997). To the extent that governments are sensitive to the discipline of global markets and locked into pursuing economic growth in a neo-liberal system, they are increasingly beholden to global finance and international financial institutions and consequently less responsive to the wishes of the electorate. In this context, governments invoke the "national interest" to support deregulation and other efforts to open national society to the global economy, and economic results – particularly the improvement of living standards and easing cost of living pressures – are increasingly crucial to state legitimacy (Carnoy and Castells 2001: 16). But this source of legitimacy is clearly a double-edged sword: while economic growth may bestow some transient form of legitimacy upon governments that pursue neo-liberal policies, it ties public support for state practices to variable economic conditions that cannot be guaranteed. This is especially problematic in the context of the financialization of global capitalism where various forms of financial instability and crisis reoccur and undermine social welfare and solidarity, as seen most graphically in the 2008 global financial crisis.

As such, there is a profound disjuncture between the historical entitlements of national citizenship and what governments can deliver in the contemporary world. There are signs that severe restrictions are in place on the "things people can expect from even the best-run government" (Cerny 1997: 258). This undermines the "symbolic social function" of the nation-state leading to

> a growing disjunction between democratic, constitutional and social aspirations of people – which are still shaped by and understood through the frame of the territorial state – on one hand, and the dissipating possibilities of genuine and effective collective action through constitutional political processes on the other. (Cerny 1996: 130–1)

This not only leads to "an erosion of the idea of a public interest," but also proves problematic for the stable reproduction of forms of political governance suitable for any form of complex social organization, not to mention a moral license for the interventionism of neo-liberal governance (Cerny 1999: 2). The ability of the nation-state to harness communal solidarity to pursue political objectives is a source of considerable power. The shift to a world of competition states casts a long shadow over this power and creates a "post-democratic" context where the democratic integrity of liberal democratic states is hollowed out (Crouch 2004; see also Gill 2012), opening up public and scholarly interest in alternatives to liberal democratic thought (Isakhan and Slaughter 2014). Competition states are increasingly constrained in their domestic public functions, but economic globalization requires the support of the rule of law, the institutional support that is rendered by states and the international institutions set up by them (Strange 1996: xii). Nation-states require the idea of national belonging and sharing a common fate to secure their legitimacy, but these sentiments are more difficult to sustain within an economic system and a pattern of governance where social life is being reduced in significant respects to efficiency and competitiveness.

These challenges are evident in the so-called "return of the state" in the early twenty-first century. The September 11 terrorist attacks and the launch of the "war on terror" by the United States have demonstrated the state's unique capacity to maintain domestic order and wage war. But the conflicts in Iraq and Afghanistan have also highlighted the importance of appeals to patriotism and national solidarity to justify the enormous costs of war and the increased surveillance and control of citizens in Western states. Furthermore, the state's vital role in economic affairs has also been recently reasserted in the economic success of states like China and the emphasis on state-building in development and peace-building initiatives in sub-Saharan Africa. These states may not strictly conform to neo-liberal ideology, but as competition states the rule of law and property rights, as well as education and training, is directed at boosting productivity and providing support for key export industries. In a similar vein, the crucial economic role of the state has been highlighted by responses to the 2008 global financial crisis and ensuing economic malaise in the West. The massive stimulus and bailout packages were funded, coordinated and implemented by states as a response to market failure on a global scale. However, state intervention has largely centred on bank bailouts to safeguard financial stability rather than social insurance for citizens adversely affected by economic turmoil not of their own making. The role of IGOs like the EU and IMF in imposing fiscal austerity on heavily indebted states like Greece in exchange for financial support also highlighted the state's inability to deliver on its promises of democratic choice, domestic economic stability and social welfare (Castells et al. 2012; Isakhan and Slaughter 2014; Gill 2012). The "return of the state" has thus revealed the serious difficulties in reconciling the social functions of the modern nation-state with contemporary neo-liberal globalization.

Public Responses to Globalization

These developments have significant implications for the practice of democracy. It is clear that the state will remain a central and consti-tutive feature of the rapidly changing global political system. But we have also witnessed the increasing political power of non-territorial forms of organization, including IGOs, TNCs, transnational social movements, and international regulatory agencies. These develop-ments have considerable political ramifications for the capacity of states to promote social justice and to recognize and advance the interest of their national populations against the interests of agencies and constituencies beyond the state. As such, concerns that power has been given to distant IGOs or private bodies that are not demo-cratically governed have provoked various forms of public concern and resistance which question the future of democracy within the nation-state (Held and McGrew 2007: 163–73). Susan Strange (1996) deftly describes this situation in *Retreat of the State* where she argues that people face "Pinocchio's problem" in a world of overlap-ping forms of authority and governance. This problem refers to the children's story where the puppet Pinocchio is turned into a real boy and suddenly has no strings to guide his actions. Without strings, he has to make up his own mind about how to live his life. Likewise, the diffusion of state power and authority has left contemporary citizens with "a ramshackle assembly of conflicting sources of authority" (Strange 1996: 199). Today's citizens all share Pinocchio's problem: the strings that bound them largely unambiguously to the nation-state have frayed and the lines of democratic representation and accountability have blurred. But once people are at least partially "freed" from the strings of the nation-state, how do they choose where their loyalty rests and develop effective and accountable forms of authority? There has been no definitive response to this question. States around the world vary in their capacity to generate democratic authority and attract widespread loyalty. Consequently, there are a variety of identifiable responses to Pinocchio's problem of political action within a context of dispersed authority and loyalty.

Broadly speaking, public responses to globalization in Western states include efforts to either transcend the state in a cosmopolitan sense or to re-entrench national identity. Mark Rupert (1997: 142) suggests that in the US during the 1990s there were at least two distinct positions: the cosmopolitan, democratically oriented left; and the nationalistic/individualistic far right. The cosmopolitan response is notable because it has been at the forefront of global forms of activism and social movements that bypass the state. For instance, many of the protests against global capitalism during the 1990s ignored the policy-making capacities of the state and instead focused upon the IFIs or advanced broader notions of "Empire" or "imperialism" that pointed to the power of unaccountable TNCs over the lives of ordinary people. These protests were significant signs of a progressive reaction against "globalization-from-above" through the operation of social movements with global connections that might be called "globalization-from-below" (Falk 1997: 19–22). In 2011, the Occupy movement refocused attention on the state, largely due to the regulatory failings that led up to the global financial crisis and the perception that representative democracy in the US (and beyond) is overwhelming influenced by the moneyed interests of Wall Street (Bray 2014). More generally, campaigns inspired by human rights and environmental movements include groups that attempt to explicitly promote social justice and democracy. While these movements do engage with the policies of states, the primary aim of campaigns on climate change or global poverty, for example, is to represent public concerns that transcend state interests and to generate action on global problems facing vulnerable people around the world. However, cosmopolitanism does not adequately capture the responses of some groups such as the *Zapatistas* in Mexico, who explicitly resist neo-liberalism but are very much embedded in local communities, despite their effective use of transnational communications (Castells 1997: 72–83; Pleyers 2010). Many of these groups feel that the nation-state has lost its traditional legitimacy and increasingly identify with sub-national forms of community.

The nationalistic far-right response involves an array of conservative groups that are suspicious of both governments and globalization. In particular, far-right reactions to economic globalization and the prospect of a world government rest on profound suspicions concerning the power of external political and economic forces and the belief that the state is complicit in allowing them to weaken or destroy the nation (Rupert 1997: 150). These groups are interesting because they exhibit the fears of a segment of a population in wealthy states that generally benefit from the operation of economic globalization. While these anti-government claims have a distinctly American cast to them, the signs of far-right politics have been evident in many places around the world. In Europe, we have also seen increased forms of xenophobia and the mobilization of right-wing groups in response to fears about Muslim immigration and refugee intakes. These extreme forms of nationalist "backlash politics" are evidence of the insecurity felt by some people buffeted by globalizing forces, which are exacerbated in times of economic crisis. Across the world there are sections of societies that seek some solace in forms of autarchic nationalism or despotism. In this context, Benjamin Barber (1998: 34–5) warns "if we cannot secure *democratic* communities to express our need for belonging, *undemocratic* communities will quickly offer themselves to us."

Responses to Globalization in Democratic Theory

Democratic theorists have responded to the dispersed authority of the state in a variety of ways. In most respects the divide between the left and right of politics has remained trenchant as ever, but the divide between nationalist and cosmopolitan arguments have become more pronounced with significant rise in cosmopolitan scholarship since the mid-1990s. While the specific approaches of global democratic theory will be outlined and examined later in this book, there are few key themes that need to be mentioned here to give a brief overview of how democratic theory has responded to the rise of globalization and the changing role of the nation-state. First, one strand of democratic theory fundamentally *assumes the existing nation-state* as the framework of analysis. Scholars such as John Rawls and Philip Pettit assume that the state remains unquestionably at the centre of political and therefore democratic life. Rawls' defence of liberalism in *The Law of the Peoples* accepts the state as central to both liberal democratic and non-liberal societies (which includes what he refers to as "burdened societies": societies living under historical, social and economic circumstances that make achieving a "well-ordered regime" difficult, if not impossible) (Rawls 1999: 90). But in assuming the state there are strong indications that Rawls is trapped in a "vanished Westphalian world" in the sense that his just state system simply replicates traditional assumptions that do not seem to cope well with the current proliferation of transnational flows and global networks (Buchanan 2000). This is indicative of scholarship with a distinctly communitarian and nationalist cast that assumes the moral and political importance of democracy within existing boundaries.

A second strand of democratic theory argues for *transcending the state*. For instance, scholars such as David Held and Richard Falk develop theories that attempt to transform the state and embed it within cosmopolitan forms of global democracy. Since the 1990s, these cosmopolitans have developed the idea that existing nation-states cannot be the basis for a just future and that the state system must be changed in order to create a more inclusive and democratic global order. These forms of cosmopolitan theory emphasize the moral and political shortcomings of the state in its capacity to address global problems given the rising significance of contemporary globalization. The intensification of globalizing trends, including the positive contributions of transnational civil society and forms of global consciousness, has been central to the cosmopolitan critique of the state system. These impulses are utilized by cosmopolitans as the political grounds for developing cosmopolitan democracy in which global institutions are directed by the political and electoral activity of all human beings. This project is ultimately focused on the creation of new global forms of democratic political community.

A third strand of democratic theory largely *ignores or bypasses the state*. All forms of cosmopolitan scholarship attempt to move beyond existing states to some degree, but this strand of democratic theory consciously seeks to shift democracy away from state institutions and therefore gives little or no account of the role of the state in emerging or proposed forms of transnational democratic practice. The work of John Dryzek (2006), for example, provides little detailed examination of the state and instead focuses upon the development of forms of global deliberation and discourse in transnational forms of civil society. These forms of democratic practice bypass the state and create new modes of political participation outside of state authority and beyond electoral conceptions of democratic practice.

Finally, a fourth strand of democratic theory argues that it is possible and desirable to *reinvigorate the state* as a locus of democratic action. While there are political discourses such as the Third Way which argue for a revival or reconstruction of the nation-state, serious questions are raised about whether such arguments are directed at reforming the state as an authentic democratic polity or merely see the state as an institutional vehicle for neo-liberal practices (see Chapter 6). There are also various attempts to conceive of "cosmopolitan states" that transcend nationalism as the foundation of law and politics in an era of globalization (e.g. Brown 2011; Glenn 2013). The key issue for democratic theorists is whether the state can be revived as a framework that develops and utilizes political power for democratic purposes, rather than for private gain of some individuals and groups. One example of such a position is Robyn Eckersley's argument for a "green state" (Eckersley 2004). Contrary to most Green political theory, Eckersley contends that the liberal state could be transformed by Green principles and environmental activism to create a state and international system able to address and moderate environmental problems. This argument rests on developing the regulatory capacities of the state, in conjunction with developing forms of "environmental patriotism" (Eckersley 2004: 231). Likewise, there has been a revival in republican arguments that seek to reconstruct the capacity of the state to promote liberty within and beyond its territory (S. Slaughter 2005, Laborde 2010). These arguments tend to support cosmopolitan arguments for stronger and more wide-ranging forms of global governance, but contend that this requires states that are animated by publics shaped by republican virtues and institutions.

Conclusion

There are a great number of questions about the feasibility and desirability of these different perspectives regarding the democratic potential of the state in light of globalization. These will be explored in later chapters, but the underlying point here is that democratic theory does not necessarily assume that the state will be the sole location of democracy. This chapter has demonstrated that democratic practices and public choice within the state are constrained by global forms of governance and the neo-liberal transformation of state capacities. It is also the case that political contestation is no longer solely focused on the policies of states. Despite these transformations, however, the agency of the state is still significant. It is important to recognize the ways in which neo-liberal globalization and the financialization of global capitalism have involved political leadership that has both required and transformed the state (Gill 2012). In this light, democratic theories need to consider how their respective visions can be implemented given the enduring significance of the state in contemporary global politics. However, they also need to address the development of global forms of governance and transnational networks of civil society. These developments have opened up important possibilities for the development of democracy beyond the state that will be examined in the next chapter.

Key Readings

Held, D., McGrew, A., Goldblatt, D. and Perraton, J. (1999) *Global Transformations: Politics, Economics and Culture*. Polity, Cambridge.

Held, D. and McGrew, A. (2007) *Globalization/Anti-Globalization: Beyond the Great Divide*, 2nd edn. Polity, Cambridge.

Sassen, S. (2006) *Territory, Authority, Rights: From Medieval to Global Assemblages*. Princeton University Press, Princeton.

Strange, S. (1996) *Retreat of the State*. Cambridge University Press, Cambridge.

Weiss, L. (1998) *The Myth of the Powerless State*. Cornell University Press, Ithaca.

2
Global Governance and Transnational Civil Society

While globalization has challenged and restricted democracy within the state, it has also changed the nature of global politics in ways that have opened up democratic possibilities. In particular, the development of global forms of governance and networks of transnational civil society have changed global politics to such an extent that the global agenda now routinely includes moral and political debates about democracy. This is a remarkable turn of events. In the 1960s, the International Relations scholar Martin Wight (1966: 26) claimed that the international realm is "the realm of recurrence and repetition" where ethical claims are limited. This argument was based on a sharp distinction between the domestic realm of "normal" politics within nation-states where ethical reflection is legitimate, and the international realm of anarchy where state survival overrides ethical purposes. As Wight explains (1966: 33):

> Political theory and law are maps of experience or systems of action within the realm of normal relationships and calculable results. They are the theory of the good life. International theory is the theory of survival. What for political theory is the extreme case (as revolution, or civil war) is for international theory the regular case.

Today, it would be a brave observer to claim that the international realm is *only* a realm of survival. In the fifty years since Wight made this claim, the international realm has clearly become more interdependent, globalized and institutionalized. Furthermore, the geopolitical tensions that underpinned the Cold War have been moderated by various forms of global dialogue that are subject to the moral and political interventions of IGOs, NGOs, and other transnational actors. Generally speaking, people are more aware of a range of cross-border social, economic and ecological problems that endanger present and future generations. In recent decades, complex forms of international cooperation and a variety of transnational social movements have been created to address these problems.

But serious questions remain as to whether the international realm is sufficiently analogous to the domestic realm to permit discussions of the "good life" or arguments for democracy at the global level. Indeed, in order to support the idea that international relations is a realm where ethical projects can be realized, it is necessary to consider how contemporary global governance shapes moral and political possibilities beyond states. In this chapter, global governance encompasses official forms of cooperation and organization established by states and the various non-state influences such as private regulation and transnational civil society, which help to establish rules that govern specific aspects of global political practice. The term suggests that the activities of states, IGOs and transnational actors are heavily intertwined in practice. As such, this chapter first examines the history of IGOs and the development of contemporary global governance. Second, it identifies the purposes and problems of contemporary global governance, including important concerns about the legitimacy of global rules and decision-making processes. The third section examines the nature of transnational civil society and the possibilities of harnessing it to democratize global institutions. Finally, the chapter examines how the relationship between democracy and global governance has become an increasingly important issue for international theorists in a rapidly expanding literature of global democratic theory.

A Brief History of Global Governance

In order to map global governance and its implications for democracy, it is first necessary to examine the meaning of the term "global governance." In a generic sense, global governance refers to cooperative problem solving and rule making arrangements for managing global processes. In a more specific sense, global governance commonly designates the system of institutionalized cooperation that emerged in the aftermath of the Second World War with the formation of the UN and a host of sector and issue-specific institutions ranging from the Bretton Woods organizations to the Intergovernmental Panel on Climate Change. Here, global governance refers to an array of disaggregated institutions established by states as well as the activity of individuals operating through NGOs, social movements, and private business associations. Governance thus suggests the forms of authority, cooperation or management – be they public or private and formal or informal – that lead to the achievement of collective goals. According to *The Commission on Global Governance* (1995: 2–3):

> Governance is the sum of the many ways individuals and institutions, public and private, manage their common affairs. It is a continuing process through which conflicting or diverse interests may be accommodated and co-operative action may be taken. It includes formal institutions and regimes empowered to enforce compliance, as well as informal arrangements that people and institutions either have agreed to or perceive to be in their interest.

While governance involves the exercise of authority, global governance does not mean global or world govern*ment*. Government generally refers to authoritative political institutions of a territorial community. Governance, however, is a broader, more encompassing phenomenon that refers to the development of common rules of cooperation underpinned by coercive force or voluntary compliance. That is, global governance refers to a variety of decision-making structures at the global level that may involve governments, but together do not amount to a centralized global government. Broadly speaking, global governance attempts to address problems that no individual state can address in isolation as well as enable productive interconnections across territorial borders, especially those needed to sustain global capitalism.

It is therefore important to recognize the role played by international treaties, IGOs and transnational actors in the architecture of global governance. International treaties are official agreements by states concerning a specific issue that are not supported by a formal organization presiding over the agreement. IGOs, in contrast, are formally established by states as legal bodies for making and enforcing cooperation. IGOs can be regional or global in scope and can regulate an entire sector (e.g. global trade), one specific issue (e.g. climate change), or sometimes multiple related issues (e.g. the UN Economic and Social Council). These organizations exist to serve state goals and can normally only make decisions with the consent of member governments. However, sometimes IGOs can acquire their own agency and hence develop interests and goals of their own. IGOs contrast with international treaties because international cooperation often outgrows international treaties administered by member states and requires an IGO with its own independent structure. This may be due to the complexity of the issue-area or the need for an autonomous actor to administer the treaty system, lead negotiations, and advance cooperation in the collective interest. A key example is the transformation of the General Agreement on Tariffs and Trade (GATT) regime into the World Trade Organization (WTO) in 1995, which supplemented the treaties with a secretariat, a dispute resolution system, a court to hear appeals, and a body to supervise national trade policies. The number of IGOs has risen dramatically since 1945 and developed forms of governance for a range of issues from international security and trade to transport and fisheries. Alongside these treaties and IGOs, global governance also involves transnational actors that operate across the territorial borders of nation-states, including NGOs, social movements, corporations, and organized business interests. As explained later in the chapter, transnational actors play a crucial role in influencing the development of the rules, ideas and policies that frame collective goals concerning the regulation of global processes.

Against this background, it is clear that global governance is a historical product of political action rather than a natural or inevitable feature of global politics. The history of interstate relations demonstrates the importance of key political actors such as great powers in creating cooperative institutions as well as shaping their continually evolving objectives. Well before the formation of the UN and Bretton Woods organizations there were significant forms of international agreement between states directed at common goals. Indeed, there are three overlapping phases where particular dynamics of governance became apparent. The first phase is evident from the 1600s in the form of international coexistence underpinned by the mutual recognition of sovereignty. Signs of a common society of states can be found in post-feudal Europe where emerging states did not merely interact with each other based on strategic considerations, but also at the level of mutual recognition, agreement and cooperation (Bull 1995 [1977]). In the seventeenth and eighteenth centuries, European states agreed that values of sovereignty and international peace should be jointly pursued so as to enable mutual coexistence. In order to maintain this coexistence, these states needed to recognize each other as members of a society of states bound by certain rules; not as isolated units in a system of states where war is ubiquitous, or as constituent parts of an empire where sovereignty is subjugated. The mutual recognition of sovereignty among European states eventually led to institutionalized practices such as diplomacy and international law that maintained order in European international society and continue to form the bedrock of international relations.

A second phase in the history of global governance is evident from the late 1860s in the form of multilateral cooperation. While the European society of states was a loosely arranged form of institutionalization, there were efforts in the nineteenth and twentieth centuries to establish more formal institutions directed at international cooperation rather than mere coexistence. In the late nineteenth century, cross-border governance tended to focus on the *low* politics of technical cooperation in response to new technologies and industries, leading to the development of the International Telegraph Union in 1865 and the European Rail Union in 1890. In the first half of the twentieth century, however, there were grander efforts and dismal failures to develop forms of global governance to assist in the *high* politics of state security and the prevention of war. Reflecting the growing influence of liberal ideas in global politics, the League of Nations was created after the First World War to manage the growing military problems of the 1920s and 30s, but ultimately failed to create a universal organization with enough power to pacify international relations or address the socio-economic malaise of the Great Depression that was generating so much domestic and international instability. The ensuing "Twenty Years Crisis" culminated in the horrors of Second World War (Carr 1946). This experience of conflict and human suffering provided a strong motivation to undertake renewed efforts to promote multilateral cooperation after 1945. Multilateralism entailed common rules and reciprocal cooperation between multiple states and culminated in the framework of post-war international institutions which had their roots in the planning for a new political and economic order that took place in the closing stages of the Second World War and led to the founding of the UN and the IMF, World Bank and (eventually) the GATT at Bretton Woods.

We can speak of international cooperation in this sense largely because of the influence of liberal ideas in global politics evident in the multilateral development of the UN and Bretton Woods institutions after the Second World War. Indeed, the UN is evidence of a widespread commitment to moderating war and promoting social and humanitarian ends more generally, and is evidence of a shift from interstate coexistence toward interstate collaboration with regards to a range of mutually valued goals. The Great Depression and Second World War provided a strong motivation to promote multilateral cooperation after 1945 in the form of IGOs set up by states. While the UN had a strong focus on preventing war in its charter and via the formation of a United Nations Security Council, its mandate also focused upon liberal commitments to promoting human rights, development and humanitarian ends (Jolly et al. 2005). These goals were pursued by a range of specialized agencies and organs on a grander scale than the League of Nations. Indeed, the UN has been described as "the most ambitious experiment to date in multilateral management of world society" (Reus-Smit 1998: 3). Furthermore, the establishment of economic institutions established at Bretton Woods have also been central to liberal efforts to support post-war international trade and global capitalism. These developments reflect a profound historical shift from interstate coexistence toward ambitious international collaboration on a range of collective goals in global politics.

During the Cold War, global forms of governance faced considerable uncertainty. Many of the UN's core goals were not effectively pursued due to the paralysing effects of superpower rivalry between the United States and the Soviet Union, particularly in the Security Council. In the 1950s and 1960s, Cold War divisions also meant the Bretton Woods organizations remained limited in scope to the Western Bloc of liberal democratic countries. Furthermore, the process of decolonization that began in this period dramatically transformed international politics and the membership of the UN by creating a host of new and economically underdeveloped nation-states. During the 1950s and 1960s, there were also new developments in regional governance such as the European Economic Community, which became the European Union (EU) in 1993. Another notable feature of this period was dissolution of the original mandate of the Bretton Woods system. In 1971, the US government under President Nixon announced that it was suspending the convertibility of the dollar to gold because of economic stagnation and high inflation in the US. This abandonment of the Bretton Woods system of fixed exchange rates precipitated a shift to a neo-liberal policy framework in the IMF and World Bank that carved out new roles in the global economy centred on structural adjustment, economic development, and poverty alleviation projects in developing countries (Cerny 1997: 259). While this system of multilateralism played a key role in enabling global interdependence, it was beset by an ever changing array of challenges.

A third phase is evident from the 1970s in the form of increasing transnational coordination which involves both multilateral cooperation and the involvement of various transnational actors and networks in global policy-making. Global cooperation clearly lies in inter-state collaboration and the growing number of IGOs creating frameworks of international law that establish principles for legitimate political action. Indeed, the number of IGOs has risen dramatically since 1945 to reach over 2000 today, reflecting an unprecedented demand for global governance institutions (Hale and Held 2011: 5). However, while sovereignty and multilateralism still influence the contours of global governance, in many respects multilateralism has been so successful in enabling interdependence and globalization among a growing number of states that this system has become overloaded and gridlocked in attempting to create mutually binding responses to a range of economic, security and ecological issues (Hale and Held 2012; Hale, Held, and Young 2013). Consequently, the greater awareness of economic interdependence between the world's major economies and concerns about the efficacy of existing forms of multilateralism in the 1970s led to the formation of new forms of governance, such as the informal Group of 7 (G7) to coordinate economic policies of the world's wealthy industrial states in North Asia, North America and Europe. The G7 expanded to the G20 leaders forum in 2008. Likewise, informal networks of states with similar interests such as the more recent BRICS arrangement comprised of Brazil, Russia, India, China, and South Africa is a coalition of states that attempt to foster cooperation between smaller groups of member states.

Alongside these developments, advances in communications technology have led to the development of forms of global governance which include non-official agents such as NGOs, TNCs, think tanks, and business groups, as well as social movements that operate within a broader transnational public sphere or civil society (Hale and Held 2012). The inclusion of these transnational actors in global governance blurs the lines between official state or IGO authorization and transnational activism (A. Slaughter 2004; Stone 2008; Hale and Held 2011, 2012). In recent decades, we have seen the rise of transnational policy networks where

> a plethora of institutions and networks negotiate within and between international agreements and private regimes have emerged as pragmatic responses in the absence of formal global governance ... This is a double devolution; first, beyond the nation-state to global and regional domains; and second, a delegation of authority to private networks and nonstate actors. (Stone 2008: 24)

In this context, a variety of transnational networks are clearly operating as forms of global governance by seeking to influence the policies of existing IGOs or indeed create novel forms of transnational rule setting and policy-making. New forms of transnational governance also include public and private arbitration bodies, multistakeholder initiatives, voluntary regulation systems and transnational financial mechanisms (Hale and Held 2011). Such arrangements include innovations such as the development of public–private partnerships such as The Global Fund to Fight AIDS, Tuberculosis and Malaria in 2002, which has outlaid more than 22 billion dollars since its establishment to tackle these diseases; and voluntary initiatives like Fair Trade and the Kimberley Process to track diamonds sourced from war zones.

In these forms of transnational governance, the state is not the primary actor involved in coordination and rule-setting, if it is involved at all. Thomas Hale and David Held (2011) have thoroughly mapped the wide array of transnational forms of governance which include public and private activity that utilize forms of arbitration, voluntary regulation and transnational financial mechanisms to influence the activity of governments, businesses and individuals. Private certification initiatives like the Rainforest Alliance, for example, are increasingly important forms of regulation that are changing political and consumer behaviour around the world. We can also see private forms of regulation in the various standard-setting agencies within global capital markets, such as the financial reporting standards contained in the International Accounting Standards Board and monetary policy issues covered by the Basel Committee on Banking Supervision (Hale and Held 2012: 170–3). These private forms of authority are frameworks that shape the rules that constitute global governance, despite not being constituted by states. The picture is complicated further when we recognize that the divide between public and private can be blurred by various forms of public–private partnership, not least in the area of international development where a host of agencies contribute (and sometimes compete) in policy-making and implementation in developing countries (Hale and Held 2011). The interaction and overlap of these official and non-official frameworks produces a complex network of political authority that reflects the variety of agents and impulses shaping contemporary global governance.

During this phase of increasing transnational coordination, global governance began to have significant impacts on economic debates, particularly with the dissemination of neo-liberal and free market policies of the "Washington Consensus" by the IMF and World Bank in the 1980s. This development had controversial impacts across the world and demonstrated the significance of thinks tanks and organizations representing transnational business interests, such as the Trilateral Commission and the World Economic Forum (Gill 1998; Harvey 2005). The influence of neo-liberal ideas was also evident in the transformation of the GATT regime into the more powerful WTO in 1995, as well as various forms of market surveillance and self-regulation evident in the rising profile of credit rating agencies such as Moody's Investors Service. For over a decade economic negotiations concerning a new "Doha Round" of trade agreements in the WTO have been stymied by a lack of international support and serious disagreements between developed and developing countries about fundamental issues like agricultural protection. Moreover, the influence of neo-liberal ideas in shaping patterns of transnational coordination has continued despite the 2008 global financial crisis and its aftermath (Gill 2012). The crisis demonstrated a failure of national banking regulation in the US and Europe and the slow and problematic nature of global forms of economic governance. There was also recognition that existing institutions such as the IMF were not only insufficiently resourced, but also did not give sufficient representation to emerging economies like the BRICS countries, especially given the rising significance of China. Consequently, the development of the G20 sought to balance representation and effectiveness by providing a forum for the leaders of the world's economically significant states to include both emerging economies and established industrial countries to coordinate their economic policies and prevent global crises.

Global governance as both international cooperation and transnational coordination has continued to be profoundly influenced by geopolitical forces and events. For example, after the end of the Cold War, the UN also increased in prominence through Security Council resolutions that allowed military intervention in Iraq in 1990–1 and the rising importance of humanitarian and human rights discourse in response to the humanitarian atrocities of the post-Cold War period. During the 1990s, the UN – supported by member states and NGOs – expanded peacekeeping operations, responded to cases of humanitarian suffering, and sought to create new institutions such as the International Criminal Court (ICC) to prosecute genocide, war crimes and crimes against humanity. New humanitarian ideas like "human security" and the "responsibility to protect" emerged through UN dialogues in this period and sought to shift the emphasis from state security to the security of individual human beings (Jolly et al. 2005). Some nation-states championed humanitarian ideas by creating the "Human Security Network," which grew out of a bilateral arrangement between Canada and Norway but expanded to include over a dozen countries from all regions of the world and some non-governmental organizations (Jolly et al. 2005: 33–4), indicating the ways in which multilateralism can intersect with transnational networks. Global cooperation was also significantly shaped by the 9/11 attacks and subsequent US-led "war on terror." Confidence in global security governance was undermined when the US and its allies bypassed the UNSC and invaded Iraq in the face of widespread international opposition and significant public protests all over the world (Hale et al. 2013: 281).

The history of global governance demonstrates overlapping logics of coexistence, cooperation, and coordination as well as the growing complexity of international institutions the global level. Frameworks of global governance are now created by the official authority of states as well as by the political action of transnational actors that establish rules governing specific aspects of global politics. These contemporary forms of global governance operate at a distance from the democratic participation and oversight of citizens, which leads to charges that these institutions have "democratic deficits." In this context, the accountability of these forms governance to people affected by the decisions emanating from these bodies is not straightforward or clear. The formal nature of multilateral IGOs may privilege government agencies involved in advancing national interests and limit transparency and responsiveness to the wider public (Steffek 2010). Conversely, the informal and voluntary nature of many transnational forms of governance may allow powerful and wealthy actors to avoid meaningful restraint in the short term. These forms of governance may be more responsive to market actors that are involved in these schemes than to any notion of the public good, and thereby be dependent on the oversight of NGOs and transnational activist networks for any form of accountability (Hale and Held 2011: 29). In this context, these forms of transnational governance and the related networks of policy-making may assist the coordination of economic and social activity in an era of globalization, but their democratic credentials are unclear at best.

The Purposes and Problems of Contemporary Global Governance

Given this complex picture, how can we make sense of the purpose of global governance and related questions of power and legitimacy? It is difficult to discern any single and specific purpose given that global governance is constituted by rules, principles and institutions created by an array of actors which possess multiple – and often contradictory – political and normative purposes. Nevertheless, it is generally held that since the end of the Second World War, liberal principles have been particularly influential in developing multilateralism and shaping the main contours of global governance in order to promote stability and address global problems. Liberalism has been prominent in official policy-making circles such as the UN system, but has also given considerable latitude to transnational actors through institutions supportive of capitalism and human rights. We can also see that liberalism has been influential in terms of economic orthodoxy, but has shifted from the Keynesian liberalism of the post-war period to the rise of the neo-liberal project in the 1980s (Harvey 2005). This form of free market liberalism led many states to embrace free trade, but also provoked concerns from some states, NGOs and other civil society groups involved in the anti-capitalist movement, which were vividly displayed at the 1999 Seattle protests against the Ministerial Meeting of the WTO. However, not all elements of global governance are consonant with liberalism and the future of liberal influence is unclear. A variety of other impulses also shape global governance, particularly in the realm of security where the military objectives of states often trump liberal concerns with the human rights of individuals (in the "war on terror," for example). Indeed, the rise of emerging economies including China and India casts an uncertain light on the future of liberalism given that these countries have different political cultures to the North American and European countries which championed the emerging liberal order in the post-war period. In this sense, the influence of liberalism may be ephemeral to other underlying political drivers.

Consequently, in order to consider the various influences operating with respect to contemporary global governance it is instructive to briefly consider the different ways in which global governance is understood in IR theory (see Held and McGrew 2002; Barnett and Duvall 2005). First, there is the realist contention that global governance is the outcome of strategic interaction between states – especially powerful states – and the divergent interests and power these states possess. Global governance, in this view, is essentially epiphenomenal to the power of states in the sense that it is a by-product of the imperatives of great powers to coordinate action in ways that serve their own interests. Non-state actors like NGOs and corporations do not substantially influence the structures of global governance and are thus largely "rule takers" rather "rule makers" (Waltz 2000). Second, there is the analytical claim of liberals that global governance is the outcome of preferences of states to pursue cooperation in order to achieve mutual gains and address common global problems that no individual state can address in isolation (Keohane and Nye 2001b; McGrew 2002a). This view maintains that NGOs and markets can influence the level of interdependence that exists between states and therefore increase incentives to cooperate. From this perspective, global governance therefore consists of structures that are at least partially independent from state interests. Third, there are various social theories of IR such as English School theory, constructivism and the various forms of critical international theory that contend that ideas, ideologies and discourses play an important role in structuring and constituting states as well as other actors and institutions in global governance (Barnett and Duvall 2005: 18–22). These perspectives place importance on the ability of non-state actors to influence states and IGOs through the development of particular norms and discourses (like human rights or sustainability) (Dryzek 2006). These perspectives emphasize the importance of political dialogue and communication with respect to the changing operation and legitimation of global governance.

Against this theoretical background of different perspectives on the dynamics shaping global decision-making, a number of problems concerning contemporary global governance can be identified. Perhaps the most important is the overarching problem of *effectiveness* in terms of preventing and addressing global problems, enabling transnational interconnections, and providing global public goods. Clearly, issues requiring collective action now extend beyond nation-states but they are often subject to weak, incomplete, or non-existent forms of global governance (Scholte 2011a: 111). David Held (2010: 143–6) calls this feature of the contemporary world the "paradox of our times" and highlights the ineffectiveness of global governance in addressing climate change, achieving the Millennium Development Goals (MDGs), and halting nuclear proliferation. These deficiencies are not surprising when we consider that practices of global governance reflect the priorities of powerful actors that dominate the creation of rules and institutions. All actors in global politics act in accordance with their own understanding of major problems and the appropriate structures needed to address them. However, they vary considerably in their capacity to force their concerns onto the global agenda and must cooperate with partner organizations in order to create lasting institutions. As such, global rules and processes are patchy and incomplete rather than a coherent and integrated system – and they fundamentally reflect the uneven capacity and willingness of state and non-state actors to pursue institutionalized cooperation in areas of shared interest. Clearly, states have the greatest resources at their disposal in enacting global governance, but non-state actors also have the capacity to influence political outcomes through agenda-setting and networks of collective action. In this regard, NGOs and TNCs have a much greater capacity to affect global politics than in the past. For example, in recent years we have witnessed the desta-bilizing impact of corporations like Lehman Brothers in the 2008 global financial crisis and the transnational activism of WikiLeaks in publicizing secret diplomatic cables.

These problems concerning the effectiveness of global governance institutions are difficult to disentangle from problems of *legitimacy*. In some cases, global governance faces significant questions about whether basic standards of justice are realized. The debates since the mid-1990s about the appropriateness of the policies and processes of the IGOs like the IMF and WTO demonstrate how many people see deep injustices in the social outcomes of global capitalism promoted by these organizations and a lack of representation by affected socie-ties (O'Brien et al. 2000; Scholte 2011a, 2011b). Legitimacy exists when an institution is considered to have the right to govern and has political support from the relevant public constituency (Reus-Smit 2007: 171). The process of legitimation involves dialogue and justification between the authority or institution in question and its relevant constituencies which involves judgments about "rightful membership" (are the relevant actors included in the institution) and "rightful conduct" (does the institution accord with prevailing normative expectations of procedural and substantive action) (Clark 2005: 25)? Legitimacy matters because if an institution does not have a significant degree of support by the relevant constituencies its authority will be compromised. A lack of legitimacy can produce a range of social costs which can adversely affect the power, effective-ness and efficiency of an organization (Reus-Smit 2007: 163–5), which can mean the institution or its supporters must spend political and economic resources to explain or articulate its policies in ways that can slow and weaken the operation of the institution. At worst, it can mean the dissolution of the institution in question.

The problem here is that the appropriate constituency for an IGO is not always clear. Much of the issue of legitimacy thus relates to identifying what community or society an actor is meant to be acceptable and appropriate to (Clark 2003: 95). We could speak of the *international* legitimacy of an IGO with respect to the states in international society, or we might refer to its *public* legitimacy with respect to the public of states that create and support the organization as well as the transnational networks of NGOs and social movements that engage with it. Indeed, the importance of public legitimation has risen in significance in light of the growing intensity of transnational forms of media and activism (Clark 2003: 95). Not only are states and IGOs not alone in making political decisions, but they increasingly have to interact with NGOs in order to work effectively and legitimately. These forms of public engagement and contestation are not only about *the level of support* for global governance agencies like the UN or G20, but more profoundly about the question of *what principles of legitimacy* should exist in global politics. While it is difficult to create a comprehensive or widely accepted list of principles to secure legitimacy, there are emerging signs that organizations in global governance are expected to be accountable to states and people they affect, actively deliberate with those states and people, and be willing to change their policies and processes to better represent the voices of the world's population and address the issues these organizations were set up to deal with.

From this angle, the issue of *reform* is another key problem in global governance. Many of the IGOs created after the Second World War have struggled to adapt to new conditions and emerging issues. Perennial efforts to reform the UN are emblematic of the difficulties associated with updating the policies, principles, procedures and membership of key global governance organs. Although the UN has updated its activities to better address civil conflicts and problems not specified in the UN Charter (such as environmental issues), it is widely argued that more reform is required to make the organization more effective and representative of the current distribution of power and resources (Held and McGrew 2007: 195–6; Mingst and Karns 2007: ch. 8). For example, it is often pointed out that the membership of the Permanent Five (P5) of the UN Security Council – the US, Russia, Britain, China, and France – reflects the power realities of 1945 rather than the contemporary geopolitical and demographic significance of India, Germany, Brazil and South Africa. From the perspective of public legitimacy, it is widely accepted that more also needs to be done to increase the involvement of NGOs and civil society in the UN (Mingst and Karns 2007: 246–7). The problem of reform is also significant in economic organizations like the WTO which has faced pressure to change its procedures to include more input by smaller, developing states and emerging powers, as well as the publics of member states (Esty 2002). Underlying these debates about what reforms should be enacted is the lack of clear consensus about how the issue of reform in global governance should be discussed and who should be included in these discussions – questions that relate to fundamental democratic questions of representation and accountability.

Most strikingly, there is a lack of leadership concerning the future of global governance. In order for governance structures like the UN to be effective there needs to be long term vision and commitment by societies, governments, and leaders toward making global governance work. This kind of vision has been in short supply in recent years. The focus has tended to be on short-term fixes and crisis-management that is doing little to create more effective governance arrangements for addressing insecurity, suffering and instability on a global scale. It is not clear what factors will prompt the world's states to act more cohesively. Leadership from NGOs and civil society can be an important impetus for reform when states are unwilling to act. It may also be the case that worsening global problems and catastrophes will provide a strong motivation. States around the world might cooperate to reform and better resource global governance, or increasingly cede sovereignty to IGOs, if global problems such as poverty, climate change, or terrorism continue to mount or have sudden or overwhelming impacts. It must be remembered that the League of Nations did not seem realistic before the First World War, and an organization like the UN did not seem feasible in 1938, so strengthening global governance may suddenly seem "realistic" if political circumstances change. Far from being purely strategic or diplomatic questions, these issues of reform and leadership with respect to global governance have a clear political and normative importance for the future of humanity and consequently are important concerns for political and democratic theory.

In summary, we can see that cooperation in global governance is a crucial element of contemporary global politics but it suffers from a range of effectiveness and legitimacy problems. It is based on both the rules and institutions created by states and a broader world of transnational activity stemming from NGOs, social movements, corporations and individuals. This makes global governance structures incredibly complex and inherently controversial policy-making arenas where questions of representation and accountability are paramount. Questions of power, legitimacy and justice have thus taken centre-stage in contemporary debates about global governance and questions about the democratic reform of these structures are becoming increasingly important in transnational civil society.

Transnational Civil Society

As indicated above, global governance includes various rules and forms of influence developed by transnational actors operating outside the authority of the state. These transnational actors include NGOs, social movements, think tanks, corporations, lobby groups, unions, religious groups, and intellectuals (Keck and Sikkink 1998: 29–31). Such groups include long-standing organizations like the International Committee of the Red Cross and more recent organizations like Greenpeace and looser networks like the anti-capitalist movements. These actors are able to operate transnationally because the development of technologies has enabled them to easily function and communicate beyond national borders. Crucially, these developments point to the existence of global or transnational civil society as a sphere of politics typified by the dispersal of information and public deliberation (Dryzek 2012, Castells 2008; Scholte 2011b). Civil society commonly refers to the existence of a domain of associational life that exists above the individual and below the state comprised of complex networks based on interest, ideas or cultural affinity. Some definitions of civil society include businesses, some others exclude them, but the emphasis is generally on political activity where people pursue various aims outside the official ambit of the state (Walzer 1995: 7). Civil society is the domain where political issues are debated, and in doing so determine what ideas become influential in political practice. Indeed, transnational civil society contains a wide variety of political perspectives ranging from radical anarchists to religious conservatives. Groups like the anti-capitalist movement, for example, seek to radically contest contemporary political structures and engage in the "politics of disclosure" which is concerned with opening up global governance (Weber 2009: 438). Some seek to pragmatically introduce ideas in the global policy-making or attempt to introduce democratic reforms into global governance, including into global markets and the supply chain of corporations (Macdonald 2010). Some groups are animated by anarchist and libertarian impulses, as evident in the leaking of diplomatic and other official information in 2010 and 2011 by the WikiLeaks network. Other more conservative activist networks actively seek to suppress attempts to entrench human rights and social justice.

While transnational forms of activism and civil society have a long history – as evident in the nineteenth century anti-slavery movement and formation of the International Committee of the Red Cross – in recent decades there has been an escalation in the presence and activity of transnational NGOs and social movements (Dryzek 2012: 102; Scholte 2011b). This appears to have resulted in a qualitative change in the ability of transnational actors to shape political agendas, foster new norms, and influence the development of formal rules in the global public sphere. A public sphere refers to the civil space of communication and dialogue in global politics enabled by various technologies, media actors and platforms, as well as the activity of transnational actors with an array of political interests (Keane 2011: 234). Although the global public sphere is far from universal or undistorted, the existence of these communicative spaces provides an opportunity for a wide range of actors to influence public opinion and play a role "educating publics about the nature and terms of dominant discourses" (Brassett and Smith 2010: 418). This global public sphere includes social media, multi-media and visual components which suggests that this realm is an "affective arena" able to shape perceptions of key global issues (Brassett and Smith 2010: 418). In this context, civil society leaders like Nelson Mandela or Al Gore play an important role as representatives of principles and struggles in transnational advocacy networks (Bray 2011). Within this sphere, furthermore, contending ideological and cultural forces often struggle for dominance to set the parameters of political life. For example, the World Economic Forum and the World Social Forum compete to set the political agenda with their contrasting interpretations of economic globalization. Alongside the anti-capitalist movement opposing neo-liberal capitalism, there are "social movements for global capitalism" that defend the prevailing form of economic globalization (Sklair 1997).

While this myriad of transnational activity points to a political realm far different to the context of interstate survival identified by Martin Wight, there are still important questions to be answered about the impact of non-state actors. It is clear that transnational civil society groups do not possess the types of coercive or financial power of states or corporations. However, Margaret Keck and Kathryn Sikkink (1998: 16–25) argue that networks of civil society have developed a variety of strategies to shift public opinion and shape global policy-making by using their *moral* influence. First and foremost, civil society networks disseminate useful information across borders about global problems, which contrasts with the information presented by state organizations or mainstream media, and seeks to demonstrate that a given state of affairs is neither natural nor accidental. Second, civil society groups also engage in the use of symbols to simplify and make a sense of situation in order to generate concern and support for the group's cause. For example, the Kony 2012 campaign used the crimes of one warlord to draw attention to the plight of child soldiers throughout the world. Third, transnational civil society actors develop alliances with IGOs and likeminded states in campaigns to pressure other decision-makers and political actors to change policy or recognize the importance of particular issues. The Make Poverty History Campaign, for example, used allies in European governments to push the idea of debt forgiveness, trade reform, and more aid at the 2005 G8 meeting. Finally, civil society groups attempt to hold policy-makers to account by publicizing the gap between declared polices and concrete action in order to shame their target into rectifying the discrepancy. The repeated calls for states to live up to the human rights conventions they have signed is a prominent example of this accountability strategy.

Recognizing these forms of influence, recent scholarship has suggested that transnational politics has moved beyond activism and is best understood as early stages of an incipient process of transnational democratization (Goodin 2010; Dryzek 2011; Keane 2011; Bray 2011; Bohman 2007; Scholte 2011b, 2014). The claim is that these transnational actors have played increasingly prominent and systematic roles in deliberating global problems and holding power-wielders to account, and in doing so have created new forms of public involvement in sites of global authority. These forms of transnational activity do not necessarily intend to create transnational democratic institutions – let alone a global electoral democracy envisaged by some cosmopolitan scholars – but they do open up more transparent political spaces for democratic communication and contestation of existing forms of governance. As Robert Goodin (2010: 179) argues, "we are still very much in the *early* days – both of developing a global polity, and still more of democratizing it. What we should be looking for in that context are 'first steps,' not final steps." From this perspective, it is necessary to recognize that even democratic practice within states involves more than elections and the activity of parliamentary representation. In many respects, democratic life increasing takes place in a range of public monitoring instruments and processes which hold power-holders to account via various forms of governmental, quasi-governmental, civil society, and media scrutiny. According to John Keane (2011), these forms of "monitory democracy" run parallel to electoral processes and often escape the confines of the nation-state.

It must be emphasized that transnational civil society will not automatically produce a global electoral democracy and it is not inevitable that these forms of public representation, contestation and monitoring will become more comprehensive or stronger in the future. Nor is there any guarantee that these forms of activity will represent all interests and voices in global politics equally. But the idea of transnational democratization suggests that a general expectation that global governance ought to be publically accountable has taken hold in civil society. It also allows us to see democracy at a global level as a gradual and emerging process. Despite representing a significant change in the nature of global politics, important questions remain about how the increased activity of transnational civil society contributes to the democratization of global governance. First, how genuinely "civil" and "democratic" is transnational civil society? There are important problems with how consistently transnational activists and transnational deliberation accurately represent those groups most affected by global decisions (Bob 2002). Second, to what extent can transnational deliberation hold official forms of global governance to account and enhance the capacity of systems of governance to make better decisions? In order to answer these questions, it is necessary to examine whether and how it is possible to strengthen the democratic credentials of transnational civil society and global governance. For this task, these questions need be considered in relation to the empirical and normative frameworks developed in global democratic theory.

Conclusion: Global Democratic Theory

In recent decades, scholars in the traditions of IR, democratic theory and political theory have increasingly reflected on the normative significance of political institutions in the context of globalization, global governance and transnational civil society. Entwined in the emergence of globalization has been a changing awareness of practical and normative interdependence in contemporary global politics. Generally speaking, people around the world are more practically interdependent in the sense that what happens elsewhere in the globe affects people in their daily practices, and people are also more morally interdependent in the sense that we are more aware of and concerned about ethical problems and suffering in other parts of the world. Consequently, there has been a revival of normative IR theory since the 1980s after its "bizarre" forty-year detour away from normative reflection during the Cold War (Smith 1992). In contrast to Martin Wight's pessimism about moral possibilities in the international realm, there is now a considerable amount of IR scholarship concerning the ethical nature of problems in global politics. In addition, while political theory and democratic theory have traditionally focused upon domestic politics and the state, they have recently taken a global turn in light of the impacts of globalization and emerging forms of regional and transnational governance. As Robert Jackson (1990: 270) claims: "political and moral theorizing on international relations is expanding, arguably because the good life is affected more and more by events external to states." In this context, "global institutions require justification just as much as domestic ones," even though there are different perspectives concerning what standards should be applied to global governance (Macdonald and Ronzoni 2012: 521). This increased focus on questions of ethics and justice has meant that democratic theory, alongside IR and political theory, has reflected on the possibilities for developing more just, representative and accountable forms of governance in the context of globalization.

Democratic reflection on global governance emerged in the 1990s in response to the impacts of globalization on democracy within nation-states. It was the cosmopolitan writings of scholars such as David Held (1995) and Richard Falk (1995) that were at the forefront of this interest in extending democracy beyond nation-states. However, there is now a large literature on rethinking democracy in a context of globalization where domestic decisions are often overwhelmed by global forces; where many see representative democracy within nation-states as a political system in crisis; and where important questions are being asked as to how citizens should relate to unelected and unaccountable forms of global governance that contain so-called "democratic deficits." This literature is best understood as "global democratic theory" and in essence centres on considering the ways in which democratic principles can be realized in a context of globalization, including by creating democracy beyond the nation-state. In an analytical sense, it involves considering the problems identified by NGOs, activists, academics and the political significance of their efforts to democratize global governance. In a normative sense, this literature develops and critically examines proposals for democratic global governance. As such, in the following chapters this book will consider the strengths and weaknesses of the most prominent liberal internationalist, cosmopolitan, deliberative, social democratic and radical approaches that engage with global governance and transnational civil society. As will become clear, these theoretical proposals have different conceptions of the core problem of democracy and different accounts of political community, the proper location of democratic authority, and how democracy ought to be institutionalized.

This chapter has demonstrated the importance of global governance and transnational civil society for understanding the problems and prospects of democracy in contemporary global politics. Underlying this chapter and the previous one is the observation that globalization and global governance are placing limits on the practice of democracy within the state. Significant elements of political life have been delegated to IGOs and global forms of governance that blur channels of representation and accountability, or remain completely closed to public scrutiny and participation. While IGOs can pursue worthy social objectives and provide global public goods, they can also pursue political programs that create social problems and advance the interests of specific groups at the expense of others. As such, public responses have been evident in the formation of transnational social movements and NGOs that provide some oversight and contestation of IGO policies and institutions. These developments have led political and democratic theory to consider the possibilities of democracy beyond the nation-state. The next part of the book examines the main approaches of global democratic theory in response to these features of globalization and global governance.

Key Readings

Hale, T. and Held, D. (2011) *Handbook of Transnational Governance Innovation*. Polity, Cambridge.

Hale, T., Held, D., and Young, K. (2013) *Gridlock: Why Global Cooperation Is Failing when We Need It Most*. Polity, Cambridge.

Keane, J. (2011) Monitory democracy. In Alonso, S., Keane, J., Merkel, W., and Fotou, M. (eds.) *The Future of Representative Democracy*. Cambridge University Press, Cambridge, pp. 212–35.

Keck, M. and Sikkink, K. (1998) *Activists Beyond Borders: Advocacy Networks in International Politics*. Cornell University Press, Cornell.

Castells, M. (2008) The new public sphere: global civil society, communication networks, and global governance. *The ANNALS of the American Academy of Political and Social Science* 616 (1), 78–93.

3

Liberal Internationalism

Since the eighteenth century, advocates of liberal internationalism have sought the creation of an international order based on the rule of law, multilateral cooperation, economic interdependence and peaceful dispute resolution between states. With the rise of international forms of governance and the entrenchment of democracy as the primary basis for political legitimacy, this project now includes promoting democratic values within a range of IGOs such as the UN and the WTO. For liberal internationalists, increased interdependence means that cooperation is required to develop global rules for managing cross-border activities that no state can manage alone. However, the traditional "club model" of international rule-making involving exclusive and opaque negotiations among state officials has become untenable because it undermines national democracy. Liberal internationalists point out that the contemporary networks of governmental actors have created regional and global processes that are not adequately transparent or meaningfully accountable to the national citizens who are bound by them. In an era of globalization, applying democratic norms to international institutions is thus necessary for safeguarding national democracy because it ensures government officials are held to account for their activities both at home *and* abroad.

This chapter analyzes the democratic ethic of reform associated with this liberal internationalist approach to global democratic theory. This approach responds to the impact of contemporary globalization by utilizing liberal democratic principles to propose reforms to existing forms of international organization, rather than to construct a global democracy with new supranational institutions that express the will of global and transnational publics. The first section examines the contemporary global governance dilemmas faced by nation-states and the eroding legitimacy of the club model due to the pluralization of politics and spread of democratic norms since the end of the Cold War. The second section uses the work of Robert Keohane, Joseph Nye and Anne-Marie Slaughter to develop a normative account of liberal internationalism that seeks to safeguard democracy at the national level by enhancing the representativeness, accountability and transparency of international institutions. This account is grounded in an explicit rejection of world government and a deep pessimism about the prospects for electoral forms of democracy at the global level. It also views capitalism as indispensable to individual freedom and human welfare, and so does not generally propose significant regulation of the global economy. As such, liberal internationalism is a reformist ethic generally supportive of global capitalist markets where democratic authority remains with constitutionally limited government officials accountable to a national *demos*. In the final section, it is argued that these liberal internationalist reforms are primarily technocratic in nature rather than substantial democratic responses to the increased power and authority of international institutions. Moreover, they present a predominantly top-down agenda that relies too heavily on the political will of liberal democratic governments.

The Globalization Paradox

Democracy has long held an important if rather ambiguous place in liberal internationalist thought. In 1917, President Woodrow Wilson famously called on the US Congress to support war against Germany to ensure that the world was "made safe for democracy." Remarkably, Wilson's call to arms also expressed sentiments of "sympathy and friendship" toward the German people. He blamed "the most terrible and disastrous of all wars" on the actions of the autocratic German government that did not reflect the will of its people. For Wilson, peace required self-governing nations where "public opinion commands and insists upon full information of all the nation's affairs" (Wilson 1917). Democracy within states, however, was not enough to transcend the *realpolitik* that precipitated war. An international concert of peace, eventually expressed in the League of Nations, was also required to create "democratic" forms of collective security based on equality and open dialogue. As Inis Claude (1971: 52) observes, Wilson fought this war to make the world safe for democracy, and he created the League to make the world safe *by* democracy. While the

failure of the League still haunts liberal internationalism, its advocates nevertheless continue to champion the idea that representative,
accountable and transparent international governance is required to
curtail the pathologies of power politics and create the conditions for
realizing democracy, capitalism and human freedom.

In recent decades, liberal internationalists have extended this
democratic ethic to a host of governance institutions that have been
created by states to manage collective problems. As globalization has
intensified and networks of interdependence have strengthened, it is
argued that international institutions are required to control conflict
and enhance coordination as the actions of governments increasingly affect their neighbours (Keohane and Nye 2001a: 1). As such,
these forms of governance must be capable of making and enforcing
common rules on a variety of cross-border activities ranging from
trade to migration. International institutions thus provide important
benefits to states because they allow them to achieve national goals
while reducing uncertainty, enhancing trust and generally minimizing
the risks of cooperation (McGrew 2002a: 274). Furthermore, transnational policy networks tend to develop within and around these
institutions, bringing together a range of public and private actors
with the power and expertise to solve collective problems. From
this angle, international regimes and their associated organizations
ranging from the EU to the International Monetary Fund, reflect the
rational choices of states and other actors concerning the collective
management of international affairs. They facilitate burden sharing,
pool valuable information, and help to discipline great powers so
that conflicts of interests can be resolved without war (Keohane and
Nye 2001b: 291–2). Consequently, these forms of governance are
generally viewed as a progressive force in international relations that
"empower states rather than shackle them" (Keohane 1984: 13). In
a world of global markets, global travel, global information networks,
of weapons of mass destruction and global environmental disasters,
"governments must have global reach" (A. Slaughter 2004: 4).

However, liberals are also traditionally suspicious of calls for
expanding the power of government and fear the oppressive tendencies of centralized political authority. This means the creation of
additional governmental functions beyond nation-states presents
a *prima facie* threat to individual liberty. Consequently, the long-
standing controversies between liberals (and their critics) about the
proper scope and ends of government have re-emerged in the past
few decades as global governance has grown and issues like human
rights, environmental protection and development aid are taken for

granted as tasks of international institutions (Steffek 2003: 29). As Anthony McGrew (2002a: 283) points out, this generates disagreement between liberal internationalists about whether global governance must be limited to dismantling barriers to individual liberty (negative freedom), or seek to regulate economic and social conditions to actively empower individuals (positive freedom). However, what is not in dispute is that some level of governance beyond the nation-state is necessary to realize liberty because in today's world individuals are subject to a host of international and transnational forces that impact on their social conditions. The key assumption is that the progressive reform or domestication of international affairs is possible through rational international cooperation that can mitigate if not transcend power politics without the forms of political centralization that lead to oppression.

The liberal internationalist account of interdependence thus suggests a "globalization paradox": we need more government at the regional and global levels, but fear the centralization of decision-making power and coercive authority so far from the people to be governed (A. Slaughter 2004: 8). As Robert Keohane (2001: 1) puts it, "although institutions are essential for human life, they are also dangerous." After the Second World War, this problem was addressed through the creation of "regimes" designed to enable government elites jointly to manage their interdependence without ceding substantial authority to international bodies. Precisely because they were weak devices for inter-state cooperation, these institutions were largely above the notice of national legislators or publics (Keohane and Nye 2001a: 2). They functioned as *clubs* of negotiators bargaining with one another within specific issue areas, often in secret, to smooth out the rough edges of policy by reducing the costs of making and enforcing agreements. As long as Western countries could negotiate exclusively among themselves in issue-areas where the fundamentals of policy were cross-nationally consistent, the effectiveness and legitimacy of the "club model" was largely unchallenged. Indeed, under the club system *a lack of transparency to outsiders* was a key to political efficacy because ministers could exclude government officials working in other issue-areas (e.g. only trade ministers have a seat at the table in WTO negotiations), and could present the public with *fait accompli* agreements, making the domestic politics easier to manage (Keohane and Nye 2001a: 4–5). However, as international regimes have strengthened and their impact on domestic politics has become more evident, they have generated intense political controversy, not least for their questionable democratic credentials.

Specifically, liberal internationalists argue that since the end of the Cold War the club system of international institutions has been undermined by two significant developments that have focused attention on its democratic deficits. First, intensifying globalization has resulted in the disaggregation and pluralization of global politics in which a greater variety of governmental actors and civil society groups seek participation in international institutions. Most prominently, many of the international regimes and organizations formerly controlled by rich Western governments have expanded their memberships to include governments from developing countries. Countries like India and China, for example, are now pivotal players in the global trade regime and have exerted increasing influence on negotiations in the WTO. Their economic significance also gives them a prominent role in newer intergovernmental institutions such as the G20. While not necessarily contesting the club-like nature of international regimes, developing countries are often suspicious of rich country leadership and resentful of the club rules created by the rich (Keohane and Nye 2001a: 7). And, crucially, the development of new rules now requires negotiation among a wider array of national interests, often generating deadlock or glacial progress in regimes ranging from trade to climate change (Hale et al. 2013). At the same time, states have become disaggregated as government officials working in specific sectors increasingly need to engage with their counterparts in global networks to solve problems, creating an increasingly dense web of transgovernmental linkages in a host of issue-areas ranging from central banking to human rights protection (A. Slaughter 2004). These networks contribute to world order by bringing together national officials to exchange information, cooperate on enforcement mechanisms, and to harmonize standards: for example, regulators cooperate to chase the subjects of regulation across national borders, judges negotiate minitreaties with their foreign counterparts to resolve complex transnational cases, and legislators consult each other to find the best ways to frame and pass legislation on human rights or the environment (A. Slaughter 2004: 12).

This disaggregated world order is further complicated by the rise of non-state actors and their claims to voice global and transnational concerns that transcend state interests. As NGOs, advocacy networks, social movements, and TNCs have become part of transnational policy networks, they increasingly perform governmental functions in providing expertise, negotiating regulations, and monitoring compliance at the international level. This has contributed to the pluralization of global politics where civil society networks contest and ally with each other and with parts of government to set agendas and press for policy change (Keohane and Nye 2001a: 13). As such, liberal internationalists see these actors as important elements of an emerging "polyarchy" in which power is dispersed in a decentralized and pluralistic system where non-state actors contribute to the responsiveness and accountability of international institutions. However, it is often also pointed out that many NGOs are self-appointed advocates or voices of special interests made up of unrepresentative elites that have little claim to democratic legitimacy. According to Joseph Nye (2003: 6), for example, some NGOs "claim to represent civil society, but represent only themselves" (see also Keohane 2003: 143–8; 2006: 80). Indeed, Martin Shapiro (2001: 369) argues that the shift from government to governance has provided opportunities for "experts and enthusiasts," the two groups outside of government with the knowledge and passion to participate in governance, but who are not representative of the larger polity. Liberal internationalist thought thus contains a profound ambivalence toward transnational civil society because it sees pluralization as a welcome development that can increase the effectiveness and legitimacy of international institutions, but also fears that power is shifting away from politically accountable national officials.

The second development undermining the club system of international governance is the spread of democratic norms. During the twentieth century, the expansion of democratically elected governments was so profound that Freedom House (1999) called it "Democracy's Century." It pointed out that in 1900 there were no states with universal suffrage and multi-party elections and only 25 "restricted democracies," including the US and UK. By the dawn of the twenty-first century, however, "liberal and electoral democracies clearly predominate[d]," with a significant expansion in the "Third Wave" beginning in the 1970s that brought democracy to much of the post-Communist world, Latin America and parts of Asia and Africa (Freedom House 1999: 2; Huntington 1991). By the end of the twentieth century, 119 out of a total of 192 countries could be described as "electoral democracies," reflecting a "growing global human rights and democratic consciousness" that has been extended to "all parts of the world and to all major civilizations and religions" (Freedom House 1999: 2). At the same time, attempts to apply democratic norms at the international level grew in significance during the 1990s with major protests in Seattle (and many other places) against the WTO that generated a "legitimacy crisis" for global economic organizations (Esty 2002). It has also been evident in the reform agenda of the UN where, for example, there are ongoing calls for the "democratization" of the Security Council by removing the veto of the Permanent 5 (P5) and expanding the membership to better represent the developing world (Mingst and Karns 2007: 239–61; Annan 2005). The key claim advanced in these contexts is that the legitimacy of IGOs now hinges on their democratic credentials. This liberal principle was put most starkly by the Commission on Global Governance (1995: 48): "it is fundamentally important that governance should be underpinned by democracy at all levels . . . as the role of international institutions in global governance grows, the need to ensure that they are democratic also increases."

From a liberal internationalist perspective, then, we are living in a post-Westphalian world where sovereignty is being reconstituted by the need for global forms of governance. However, the club model of secret and exclusive rule-making among industrialized states is no longer tenable due to the plurality of governmental and non-governmental actors that participate in and are affected by international regimes and the ascendancy of democratic norms as the primary basis for political legitimacy. Furthermore, a disaggregated world order has emerged in which transgovernmental networks interact with a wide range of non-state actors to create and enforce global rules. These processes are often opaque to national publics and involve officials, experts and enthusiasts operating outside of traditional lines of electoral accountability. As such, the voice of the people is much softer and less likely to be heard than the voices of negotiators, advocates, judges, ministers, and heads of state (A. Slaughter 2004: 104). The liberal internationalist challenge is therefore to create global rules without centralized power but with government actors who can be held to account through a variety of political mechanisms and with responsibility to multiple constituencies rather than private pressure groups (A. Slaughter 2004: 10, 257). This constitutes a reformist project that requires applying the procedural standards of democracy to international institutions to ensure that, as governments gain global reach, they remain democratically bound to national publics.

Government Networks and Democracy-Enhancing Multilateralism

As a normative approach, liberal internationalism thus seeks a world order based on the rule of law and representative government in which international institutions reflect the cooperative priorities of states and are transparent and accountable to national publics. This account of global democratic theory is premised on an understanding of democracy as a constitutionally limited political system tied to a territorially defined people. Robert Keohane and Joseph Nye (2001a: 11–12), for example, argue that while democracy generally entails "government by officials who are accountable to a majority of the people," this system can only properly function within nation-states: "meaningful voting, and associated democratic political activities, occurs within the boundaries of nation-states that have democratic constitutions and processes." Specifically, for democracy to work well "the people" must regard themselves as a political community, have a corresponding public space for discussion, and have institutions linking the public, through elections, to governing organizations (Keohane and Nye 2001a: 11). And, crucially, constitutional structures are required to provide settled rules to establish elections, to determine eligibility for voting and service in office, to define the responsibilities of various elected officials, and to govern the appointment of nonelected officials (Keohane et al. 2009: 5).

This liberal account has two related implications for the normative possibilities of global governance. First, world government is considered unfeasible because of the variety of cultural practices and political-economic preferences, the difficulties of cross-cultural communication, and competition among ruling elites (Keohane and Nye 2001a: 1). However, even if this heterogeneity could be overcome, a global leviathan is inherently undesirable because "the size and scope of government presents an unavoidable and dangerous threat to liberty" (A. Slaughter 2004: 8). Second, the lack of a global political identity or community rules out applying the "domestic analogy" of liberal democracy to global governance. According to Anne-Marie Slaughter (2004: 8), the diversity of peoples to be governed makes it impossible to conceive of a global *demos*. Indeed, any vision of a global society is a "mirage" because "national identities are unlikely to dissolve into a sense of larger community that is necessary for [electoral representative] democracy to thrive" (Keohane 2001: 9; Keohane 2003: 136). This means proposals to create a global parliament elected by the entire world population are destined to fail because without a strong sense of global community the citizens of nation-states would not be willing to be continually outvoted by a billion Chinese and a billion Indians (Keohane and Nye 2001a: 12).

This rejection of global democratic government can also be found in the normative theory of John Rawls. In *The Law of Peoples*, Rawls' starting point for developing an ideal account of international relations is to examine the institutional, cultural and moral features of territorially defined "peoples." He argues that liberal peoples (not the states that represent them) have conceptions of right and justice that permit stable, fundamental interests: "they seek to protect their territory, to ensure the security and safety of their citizens, and to preserve their free political institutions and the liberties and free culture of their civil society" (Rawls 1999: 29). In this view, global justice requires a "Law of Peoples" acceptable to both constitutional liberal democratic and non-liberal but "decent" peoples, each with their own internal governments and territorial claims. According to Rawls (1999: 3), "decent peoples" describe "nonliberal societies whose basic institutions meet certain specified conditions of political right and justice (including the right of citizens to play a substantial role, say through associations and groups, in making political decisions) and lead their citizens to honor a reasonably just law for the Society of Peoples." This Law of Peoples allows for various cooperative associations and federations based on sovereign equality and non-intervention, but does not affirm a world-state, democratic or otherwise. Following Immanuel Kant, Rawls (1999: 36) believes that a world-state would either be a global despotism or else would rule over a fragile empire torn by frequent civil strife as peoples tried to gain their political freedom and autonomy. This puts Rawls firmly in the liberal internationalist tradition.

For liberal internationalists, IGOs lack the key features that make electoral democracy possible, yet their practices and outcomes need to meet broadly democratic standards in order to be legitimate. How is this seemingly inconsistent imperative to be realized? As indicated above, the primary normative response is to welcome pluralization of global governance but enhance its democratic credentials to ensure national publics can exercize popular control over decisions. For the most part, this means ensuring that international institutions have transparent procedures and arrangements that facilitate accountability. From this perspective, democratic legitimacy is generated at the international level through "voluntary pluralism under conditions of maximum transparency" where the governance activities of national officials and civil society groups can be publicly judged and held to account (Keohane 1998: 94). While transnational civil society actors are important "pressure groups" in global governance, the liberal internationalist vision preserves a key legitimating role for national officials that can speak directly to domestic publics and act as intermediaries between ordinary citizens and international institutions. As

Anne-Marie Slaughter (2004: 234) puts it, "national governments and national government officials must remain the primary focus of political loyalty and the primary actors on the world stage."

Clearly, promoting accountability is the centrepiece of the liberal internationalist agenda to increase the legitimacy of global governance and safeguard national democracy. To clarify how this might take shape, Robert Keohane (2003) has introduced an important distinction between "internal" and "external" accountability. Internal accountability involves an institutional linkage between a principal and an agent established through authorization or support. That is, accountability is an internal relationship because the principal is providing legitimacy (authorization) or financial resources (support) to the agent. In this view, global economic institutions such as the World Bank are in fact highly accountable because they are internally answerable to the states as the principals that empower and support them. For Keohane (2003: 141), however, the most serious normative problems arise with "external accountability": "accountability to people outside the acting entity, whose lives are affected by it." In situations where international institutions are "choice-determining" for people (for example, where African farmers suffer or prosper as a result of World Bank policies), Keohane (2003: 141) asks: "should the acting entity be accountable to a set of people it affects?" This is an important question because a high degree of internal accountability (say, to donor states in the World Bank) may serve to prevent meaningful participation by those affected by the rules or due consideration of their interests (Buchanan and Keohane 2006: 426). Indeed, Jens Steffek (2010: 46) argues that "the core of the democratic deficit of international governance is a lack of accountability *to the wider public*." In the long run, Keohane (2003: 154) believes that "global governance will only be legitimate if there is a substantial measure of external accountability." But in the absence of a global constitutional system, powerful actors will always be able to avoid being externally accountable (Keohane 2003: 141). And without a stronger sense of global community, global representative democracy is out of reach as a solution.

In this context, Keohane suggests we focus on bolstering forms of accountability that already exist in global politics. Together with Ruth Grant, he outlines a variety of non-electoral mechanisms that serve to constrain abuses of power without centralized government: *inter alia, supervisory* accountability in which states, NGOs and IGOs monitor and publicize each other's activities; *market* accountability in which firms and governments can be punished for bad behaviour by investors or consumers; *peer* accountability through professional norms and transnational networks that, for example, can constrain the conduct of judges and central bankers (Grant and Keohane 2005: 35–7). These mechanisms rely on the development of international standards, sanctions and information that allow actors to hold each other to account without the participation of those directly affected in majoritarian decision-making. This constitutes a "pluralistic accountability system" to match the decentralized and pluralistic nature of governance in global politics (Keohane 2006: 84). These mechanisms can provide important external constraints on an agent's behaviour, but their *democratic* credentials are questionable because the link between popular activity and policy is severely attenuated by limited public involvement, and the fragmentation and disarticulation of accountability procedures themselves (Keohane and Nye 2001a: 14). Indeed, most of the demands for external accountability made against states and intergovernmental organizations emanate from NGOs and advocacy networks *on behalf of* affected citizens (Keohane 2003: 143; 2006: 84).

As such, liberal internationalists emphasize the need for democratic states to exert control over IGOs through chains of delegation linked to electoral forms of accountability. A common proposal is to strengthen the roles of national *politicians* with an electoral mandate either in their direct participation in global governance or through delegated officials answerable to them. Indeed, legislators have been "lagging behind" in developing international networks and can act as important correctives to the technocratic control of global organizations through the creation of assemblies of national parliamentarians, or increased domestic regulation and monitoring of executive-branch officials involved in governance activities (A. Slaughter 2004: 104–165). According to Keohane and Nye (2001a: 23), the lack of intermediating politicians with electoral mandates is "the most serious 'democratic deficit' of IGOs." Since the primary components of democratic legitimacy remain at the domestic level, it is argued that the activity of broadly based politicians speaking directly to domestic publics can have a legitimating effect on IGOs. That is, "there is a need for the involvement of politicians who can link specific organizations and policies with a broader range of public issues through electoral accountability" (Keohane and Nye 2001a: 23). This requires national officials to learn to think globally and balance the global and national interest in their policy-making roles (A. Slaughter 2004: 234–5). In this sense, national politicians can be intermediaries between organizations and constituencies: politicians channel up the concerns of their electorates during international deliberations, while remaining accountable to them for the policies they endorse in transparent procedures that allow publics to judge their performance.

As well as increasing the involvement of national politicians to bolster the legitimacy of IGOs, liberal internationalists also argue that participation in multilateral institutions can enhance the quality of *domestic* democracy. Specifically, involvement with multilateral processes often helps domestic democratic institutions restrict the power of special interest factions, protect individual rights, and improve the quality of democratic deliberation (Keohane et al. 2009: 2). That is, multilateralism is democracy-enhancing when it supports general public majorities rather than organized special interests groups. For example, institutions such as the WTO and NAFTA "provide mechanisms by which democratic publics can limit the influence of minority factions by committing in advance to a set of multilateral rules and practices that reflect broad public interests" (Keohane et al. 2009: 11). Democracy-enhancing multilateralism is also evident when institutions are developed to protect individual or minority rights in existing democracies (e.g. the European Convention on Human Rights) or by assisting non-democratic countries to make difficult transitions to more democratic governments (Keohane et al. 2009: 4–5; Dahl 1999: 32). And since international institutions are crucial for citizens to achieve security, welfare and other public purposes, failing to delegate some authority to multilateral institutions can actually place restrictions upon on national democratic deliberation. That is, far from degrading national democracy, pooling and delegating sovereignty "expands the scope of democratic choice and improves democratic control over policies that actually affect citizens, as along as procedures adhere to basic democratic standards (Keohane et al. 2009: 4–5).

The democracy-enhancing interplay of domestic and international institutions is also a central feature of Anne-Marie Slaughter's solution to the "globalization paradox." She advocates a "new world order" based on government networks that work alongside or in place of more traditional IGOs (A. Slaughter 2004). This disaggregated order would involve coordination and harmonization of national government action while also initiating and monitoring solutions to global problems. Today, many horizontal networks exist that bring together national regulators, judges and legislators in issue-areas ranging from antitrust regulation to law enforcement. Vertical networks are also evident where national governments have ceded authority to "higher" organizations, and national and supranational officials must cooperate to implement supranational rules and decisions (e.g. in the European Union, cooperation between national courts and the European Court of Justice (ECJ) is required to enforce Europe-level judgments). In order to democratize this disaggregated system, we must recognize "all government officials as performing a domestic and international function" for which they must be held to account by national constituents (A. Slaughter 2004: 28).

Keenly aware that government networks can be made up of unelected officials operating in informal settings, Anne-Marie Slaughter (2004: 244–57) proposes five liberal norms designed to ensure "an inclusive, tolerant, respectful and decentralized world order": (1) *Global Deliberative Equality*, a principle of maximal inclusion for all relevant and affected parties in processes of transgovernmental deliberation; (2) *Legitimate Difference*, a principle of pluralism that recognizes the validity of each actor's approach, as long as they all accept a core of common principles; (3) *Positive Comity*, a principle of affirmative cooperation where consultation and active assistance is substituted for unilateral action and non-interference; (4) *Checks and Balances*, a principle of separation of powers where every element of power in the world order must interact and limit each other; and (5) *Subsidiarity*, a principle of governance that locates decision-making at level closest to the people affected by rules and decisions. In this new world order, government networks ought to adopt these norms and operate as the spine of broader policy networks, including IGOs, NGOs, corporations, and other interested actors, "thereby guaranteeing wider participation in government network activities but also retaining an accountable core of government officials" (A. Slaughter 2004: 29). The use of transgovernmental networks in this way would reassure many domestic publics and would likely "keep coercive power in the hands of those [national] officials who can use it most democratically and effectively" (A. Slaughter 2004: 161).

To address some of the accountability problems posed by transgovernmental networks, A. Slaughter (2003, 2004: 156–9) proposes the creation of "global information agencies." Drawing on the EU committee system that performs advisory, management and regulatory functions between the European Commission and the Council of Ministers, she argues that "regulation by information" is a suitable ethic for global governance in which access to credible information, rather than command and control techniques, is central to changing the calculations and choices of government actors (A. Slaughter 2003: 1059). To ensure that networks of national officials behave in a similar manner, they need a structure to manage the interaction among members and a base of mutual information with which to define common problems and the range of possible responses. Global information agencies would fulfil this function by collecting, coordinating and disseminating information needed by policy-makers, thereby exercising influence through "knowledge and persuasion" (A. Slaughter 2003: 1062). Because the information and associated policy analyses would be publicly available, these agencies would bolster the democratic legitimacy of transgovernmental networks by enhancing transparency and providing a resource for judging the actions of government officials. They would also expand the representative basis of the transgovernmental networks by including private actors and "epistemic communities" to pool information in a policy area (A. Slaughter 2003: 1058–65; Haas 1992). In these disaggregated forms of democracy, government officials would have loyalty to both their national constituents and to the need to solve a larger problem in the interests of people beyond national borders (A. Slaughter 2003: 1075). Accountability would entail "a grab-bag of domestic political measures" and transparent international procedures directed at ensuring citizens have adequate information about the international activity of officials so they are able to monitor and sanction them (A. Slaughter 2004: 29; 241–4).

Global Technocracy or Democratic Internationalism?

The liberal internationalist emphasis on procedural reforms to global governance reveals an ethic of incremental adaptation rather than radical change. Its response to increasing interdependence is to reinforce the democratic control of elected governments and national publics by extending the procedural standards of liberal democracy to international institutions. Contemporary liberal internationalism does not propose any overarching political institutions to develop and express the will of a transnational or global public, or specify any wholesale changes to capitalism or inequalities of power in global politics that seem problematic from a democratic point of view. It also assumes that a collective of democratic states facing the same imperatives to cooperate in achieving national goals will drive the democratization of global governance. As such, liberal internationalism is a highly state-centric and Western approach to global democratic theory that faces significant challenges to its normative appeal and political feasibility. The central problem of this approach is that it characterizes accountability in legal and technocratic terms which does not actively entail or encourage public participation. It rests upon a top down agenda which relies upon the agency of elites in leading democratic states rather than the political activity of their respective publics, let alone transnational civil society.

From a normative perspective, liberal internationalist reforms reflect a highly restricted and primarily technocratic approach to democracy at the global level. Indeed, as Anthony McGrew (1997: 245) puts it, they reveal "the liberal fascination with constitutional and legal solutions to problems which are essentially political in nature." The drift of power and authority to unelected global technocrats who might share a functional worldview in central banking or environmental regulation, for example, but are highly disconnected from national publics prompts calls for more transparency and accountability in chains of delegation, rather than for more direct citizen participation in international decision-making. Liberal internationalism thus entails a form of "enlightened elitism" where global governance reflects transparent technocratic negotiations rather than the political choices of democratic publics. Increasing transparency and access to information, however, are not sufficient remedies to democratic deficits without also promoting citizen engagement with global governance. As Joseph Weiler (1999: 349) argues in the EU context, transparency and freedom of information are important, but "if you do not know what is going on, which documents will you ask to see?" Liberal internationalists assume national publics will be sufficiently engaged to hold their officials to account at the ballot box for their international activities without providing any other channels for participating in global governance.

The technocratic orientation of liberal internationalism is also evident in the emphasis on accountability. At a conceptual level, democracy beyond the nation-state tends to be a truncated combination of liberal pluralism and mechanisms of accountability without the requirements of electoral politics. Democracy thus entails procedures for making national officials responsible for the choices delegated to them, stripping democracy of *ex ante* channels of public voice that are required for any meaningful process of democratic self-governance. That is, since democracy is defined in terms of accountability, there is little generative role for citizens in global governance. National democratic publics cannot actively shape their social conditions; they can only react to or punish their political leaders that determine them on their behalf (Bray 2011: 10). Some liberal internationalists do not view this as a major problem because the patterns of delegation observed in EU transgovernmental networks, for example – including those that insulate certain decisions from democratic majorities in central banking, constitutional adjudication, criminal and civil prosecution, technical administration and economic diplomacy – are consistent with the general practice of most modern democracies in carrying out similar functions (Moravcsik 2002: 613, 622). This view reflects a strong faith in existing practices of liberal democracy at the national level and their unproblematic extension to global governance.

In this regard, liberal internationalists tend to see the expansion of global capitalism as a benign development from a democratic perspective, even though economic globalization has been the most important factor in transforming the policy choices available to liberal democracies in recent decades. Indeed, liberal internationalism contains a deep tension in its approach to global capitalism: it recognizes (and often celebrates) the increased prominence of market forces in recent decades, especially since the rise of neo-liberalism, yet is highly reticent about any reform or regulation of the global economy in the public interest (S. Slaughter 2005). Consistent with traditional liberal thought, democracy is confined to a political sphere that is sharply demarcated from economic life. The central dilemma for liberal internationalists, then, is what to do about neo-liberal forms of capitalism that are ambivalent, if not openly hostile to democracy and the regulation of the global economy. As outlined in Chapter 1, in recent decades neo-liberal policies in Western states have successfully limited union power; reduced marginal tax rates; rolled back welfare entitlements; privatized public enterprises; and loosened regulations on finance and commerce. This has transformed liberal democracy by narrowing democratic choice through the introduction of market rationality into public policy, increasing corporate influence in shaping political and policy agendas, and increasing economic inequality that undermines democratic processes. Against this background, those critical of neo-liberalism and capitalism argue that liberal internationalists tend to overlook the way in which inequalities of power, access and influence at home make national democracies captive to powerful vested interests and the way in which these problems are replicated or indeed aggravated at the global level (Callinicos 2003; see Chapter 6). For example, transnational civil society groups claiming to represent various public interests cannot match the resources and influence of TNCs in transnational policy networks. In a world of global capitalism, democracy beyond nation-states appears severely hamstrung if it is limited to minor institutional reforms to enhance the transparency and accountability of government networks in a narrowing political sphere that leaves markets to their own devices (see S. Slaughter 2005).

Finally, liberal internationalists present a top-down agenda that relies on the political will of liberal democratic governments, primarily the United States, to drive the spread of democratic institutions. For example, Daniel Deudney and G. John Ikenberry (2012) advocate an American grand strategy of "democratic internationalism" for an era in which the US is no longer exceptional or indispensable as an agent of liberal democracy. This grand strategy is focused on "initiating a new phase of liberal internationalism that renews and deepens democracy globally, prevents democratic backsliding and strengthens and consolidates bonds among democratic states" (Deudney and Ikenberry 2012: 1). The strategy is underpinned by the "democratic peace thesis": the claim that liberal democratic states have created their own separate zone of peace and this peace can be expanded as liberal democracy spreads throughout the world (Doyle 1986). Recognizing the problems posed by neo-liberalism, democratic internationalism proposes a return to the social underpinnings of liberal internationalism to both redress the imbalances between "fundamentalist capitalism and socioeconomic equity within the democratic world" and create a "posthegemonic system of global governance in which the United States increasingly shares authority *with other democracies*" (Deudney and Ikenberry 2012: 1, emphasis added). Since the world of democracies is threatened less by "external adversaries and ideological challengers than by problems with modern democracy itself," liberal internationalism needs to strengthen the existing democratic community by "getting its own house in order" and overcoming divisions between older Western and newer postcolonial democracies (Deudney and Ikenberry 2012: 5, 19). In this project of global democratic renewal, the US is uniquely positioned to lead international coalitions to promote democracy through *attraction* rather than coercion, even though (or perhaps because) the global distribution of power is shifting away from the West. By promoting equality of opportunity and building new and experimental international institutions through collaboration and reciprocal agreement, the community of democratic states can effectively lead global efforts to solve problems, and in doing so increase the likelihood that nondemocratic countries like China and Russia will choose engagement and democratization rather than revisionist agendas (Deudney and Ikenberry 2012: 19).

This reorientation of US foreign policy addresses some of the deficiencies of contemporary liberal democracy and their impact on promoting democracy abroad, but its emphasis on democratic reform in the West and building an international community of democratic states means it is a primarily top-down agenda that faces serious obstacles as a path of global democratization. First, it relies on an uncertain commitment by Western governments to reform liberal democracy along social democratic lines. Given the ongoing prevalence of neo-liberal agendas in many Western governments (especially in the US) and their resistance to campaigns like the Occupy movement which are critical of neo-liberalism (Bray 2014), any changes in this regard are unlikely to come about in the near future or through government-directed reforms. Second, even if projects of social liberalism and social democracy could be significantly advanced within Western states, it assumes the power of attraction will be enough to strengthen the hand of democratic reformers in authoritarian countries against the increasing power of the state apparatus in places like China and Russia. Finally, the nature of the "new and experimental institutions" and their democratic credentials are left unspecified, but they are crucial to advancing domestic democracy and creating rules for solving global problems. As such, liberal internationalist projects to reform institutional structures through state consent rely on an elite-led process and overlook the need to create a *political* constituency for democratic change that can harness the power of their civil societies.

This liberal internationalist outlook reflects the previously mentioned ambivalence toward civil society groups and their democratic role in global politics. As NGOs, advocacy networks, and social movements have become part of transnational policy networks they have contributed to the pluralization of global politics, but without the representative legitimacy of elected politicians. Indeed, for liberal internationalists, civil society groups cannot have traditional representative functions because the right to speak and act on behalf of a democratic constituency is firmly tied to elected politicians and their official delegates. In this view, the role of citizens in domestic civil society is to authorize and hold to account national officials, and the role of transnational civil society groups is limited to facilitating accountability by gathering information and disseminating it to national citizens, and pressuring states and intergovernmental organizations to abide by democratic standards of transparency and responsiveness. Therefore, in contrast to theories in subsequent chapters, civil society is not considered the primary locus of democracy or the main driver of democratization. The democratic reform of global governance is a task for representative national officials with an electoral mandate.

Conclusion

Liberal internationalism entails a strong commitment to liberal democracy at home but an attenuated democratic ethic at the international level. This agenda can been identified in the liberal scholarship concerning how governance ought to respond to globalization, as well in the influence of liberal principles on the practice of contemporary global governance. Its reform ethic is based on creating accountable global governance without the dangers of political centralization. In an era of globalization, the club model is no longer legitimate and it is therefore necessary to apply democratic norms to international institutions to ensure government officials are held to account for their activities both at home and abroad. This enables and in at least some respects safeguards the mandates of national democracies, from which all legitimate governance is delegated, without the need to create new constitutional institutions at the global level that represent the will of transnational and global publics. In the next chapter, we address the approach of cosmopolitan democracy, which sees liberal internationalism as an inadequately conservative response to globalizing forces and interdependence. Cosmopolitans seek to develop a new global architecture of institutions based on human rights and democratic values in order to entrench autonomy in an era of globalization.

Key Readings

Deudney, D. and Ikenberry, G. J. (2012) *Democratic Internationalism: An American Grand Strategy for a Post-Exceptionalist Era*. Council of Foreign Relations, New York.

Keohane, R. O. (2006) Accountability in world politics. *Scandinavian Political Studies*, 29 (2), 75–87.

Keohane, R. O., Macedo, S., and Moravcsik, A. (2009) Democracy-enhancing multilateralism. *International Organization* 63 (1), 1–31.

McGrew, A. (2002) Liberal internationalism: between realism and cosmopolitanism. In Held, D. and McGrew, A. (eds.) *Governing Globalization: Power, Authority and Global Governance*. Polity, Cambridge, pp. 267–89.

Slaughter, A. (2004) *A New World Order*. Princeton University Press, Princeton and London.

4

Cosmopolitan Democracy

The cosmopolitan ideal that individuals have common rights that accrue to them as human beings, or as citizens of the world, has a 3,000-year history stretching back to ancient Greece. However, democracy did not carve out a place in cosmopolitan theory until relatively recently. Indeed, the cosmopolitan ideal was often thought to be irreconcilable with democracy and its traditional connection with a territorially bounded polity that prescribes different rules for relations between fellow nationals and outsiders (Benhabib 2009). Even in recent times, many cosmopolitans have considered world citizenship to be a moral standard to guide political practice rather than the basis for a political system of global democracy (Linklater 1998a; Pogge 2002). In the contemporary era of globalization, however, an increasing number of cosmopolitans have argued that democratic politics must be extended to the global level to realize cosmopolitan ideals of freedom, world citizenship, and human rights. Like liberal internationalists, they argue that globalization poses serious threats to national democracy and stress the importance of constitutional solutions underpinned by the rule of law. However, cosmopolitan democrats see the overly proceduralist and statist approach of liberal internationalism as being inadequate under conditions of globalization. Cosmopolitan democrats contend that safeguarding the democratic freedoms of individuals requires more than merely enhancing the accountability of national officials or making global governance more transparent; new institutions beyond the nation-state are needed to express the will of global and transnational publics in managing complex processes of globalization.

This chapter explores a range of cosmopolitan perspectives that advocate a new global architecture of democracy. These perspectives are grounded in a universal ethic of humanity that posits the moral equality of all human beings and the creation of a global constitutional order based on human rights and cosmopolitan political institutions. The central normative claim of cosmopolitan democrats is that democracy must be extended into the global sphere to safeguard autonomy by creating communities made up of all those affected by a decision or policy. The first section examines the key "disjunctures" associated with globalization and the reconfiguration of power and authority that have undermined the assumption of symmetry between decison-makers and affected citizens that underpins traditional democratic theory. The second section examines the normative arguments of David Held, Daniele Archibugi, and Richard Falk for globalizing structures of democratic action, including the creation of a global parliament that would both "tame" globalization and transcend the anachronistic "fiction" of national sovereignty. Finally, the chapter argues that while the goals of cosmopolitans are compellingly articulated, less attention has been devoted to the political pathways that could lead to a global democratic order. The failure to couple the cosmopolitan institutional ideal to pathways of democratization results in an approach that might be normatively attractive to many liberals, but has limited usefulness in guiding social movements struggling for the democratization of existing global governance.

Globalization and the Erosion of Democratic Autonomy

Cosmopolitan democrats argue that contemporary globalization has eroded the democratic arrangements of nation-states to such an extent that we need to rethink the very nature of democracy. Throughout the nineteenth and twentieth centuries, democratic theory and practice was constructed on national foundations in which there is a "congruent" or "symmetrical" relationship between decision-makers and the recipients of decisions within a delimited territory (Held 1995: 18). Because decison-makers and their constituents were assumed to reside within the same territorial jurisdiction, it was possible to think of citizens as democratic agents capable of determining their own fate by authorizing national representatives through the ballot box and holding these representatives to account for significant decisions affecting their lives. In a world of regional and global interconnectedness, however, the outcomes of decisions often stretch beyond national frontiers. For example, motorists around the world impact on carbon concentrations in the atmosphere that produce problematic sea level rises for Pacific Island countries. Consequently, political communities can no longer be characterized as "discrete worlds" that are independently capable of determining their own future. For David Held (2006a: 292), this breakdown of symmetry between decison-makers and affected citizens has troubling implications for the key democratic ideas relating to the scope of public deliberation, representation, and accountability.

Specifically, the democratic state has become enmeshed in overlapping political structures where effective power is shared and struggled over by diverse forces and agencies at national, regional, and international levels (Held 2000: 26). According to Held (1995: 99–140), this results in major "disjunctures" between our traditional conceptions of a sovereign democratic state and the actual processes of globalization that limit the options of individual states and transform the possibilities of a democratic polity. First, the development of international law has placed individuals, governments, and NGOs under new systems of legal regulation that transcend national sovereignty (e.g. the Universal Declaration of Human Rights). Second, the vast array of international regimes and organizations has led to an internationalization of political decision-making where the power of even the greatest states comes to depend on cooperation with others for its successful execution (Held 2003: 467). Third, the position of an individual state in the global security hierarchy and the need for collective defence arrangements to coordinate technological development, arms production, and intelligence gathering, for example, imposes constraints upon the foreign policies which governments may pursue and challenges the idea of national security. Fourth, developments in communication technology and the globalization of media have created a pull between national identities and globalized cultural practices that threaten the cultural hegemony of the nation-state. Fifth, the enmeshment of national economies in global economic transactions has shifted the balance of power in favour of capital, forcing nation-states to tailor their economic programs to the anticipated responses of global markets (Held et al. 1999: 74). And finally, environmental problems such as the degradation of global commons and transboundary pollution create fundamental pressures on the efficacy of the nation-state and national democracy to respond to these pressures (Held 2000: 23–4).

According to cosmopolitan democrats, these disjunctures suggest a reconfiguration of power and authority that has strongly augmented the importance of external influences within all states (Archibugi 2008: 55). Crucially, this has decreased the areas in which a state's political community can make autonomous decisions, thereby curtailing the capacities of state-based democracy (Archibugi 2004: 443). That is, the operation of states in an ever more complex global system both affects their autonomy by changing the balance between costs and benefits of policies, and their sovereignty by altering the balance between national, regional and international legal frameworks and administrative practices (Held 2000: 27). Cosmopolitan democrats thus argue that we live in a world of "overlapping communities of fate" where national fortunes are tightly entwined and constituencies for developing and implementing policy in areas ranging from the spread of AIDS to the stability of financial markets spill over and cut across national boundaries (Held 2004: x). These developments serve to constrain national governments and blur the boundaries of domestic politics, raising serious questions about the extent to which consent, legitimacy, and accountability can be secured through national elections under globalized conditions of political decision-making.

Against this background, cosmopolitan democrats argue that the foundations and prospects of the democratic polity must be re-examined. Increasingly, national democratic publics seem like shrinking islands of autonomy in a sea of complex cross-border flows, forcing us to ponder whether the nation-state is the single and most appropriate shell for democracy (Bray 2011: 3). Held (2000: 28) argues that "the idea of a democratic order can no longer be defended as an idea suitable to a particular closed political community or nation-state." Daniele Archibugi (2008: 53) proposes that we abandon the "fiction" of the sovereign state system of autonomous political communities isolated from each other that has accompanied democratic theory since its origin. While all states are intrinsically shaped by external influences, Archibugi (2008: 56) argues that contemporary globalization causes problems for the democratic state because it distorts its internal "democratic pact" based on principles of nonviolence, popular control, and political equality. The principle of nonviolence is increasingly weakened when external disputes are resolved through diplomacy, intimidation, or war rather than constitutional processes. When a democratic state is oppressed by another community, it can no longer meet democratic commitments to its citizens, and when a democratic state decides to impose its will on others (as in the US decision to invade Iraq in 2003) it forgoes its own constituent democratic principles. A people that oppresses other peoples cannot be fully democratic (Archibugi 2008: 57). In terms of popular control, those holding public posts can be constrained if they are inside a community, but not when they are increasingly located outside of it. And the principle of political equality is over-shadowed when only a few of the persons affected by a particular decision have a say in the decision-making process. From this angle, nation-states are increasingly confronted with external pressures that undermine their ability to maintain democratic arrangements that underpin the constitutional pacts with their political communities.

Moreover, these challenges to the viability of the democratic state are particularly troubling for cosmopolitan democrats because they compromise the social democratic project of the post-Second World War period. Traditionally, social democrats have relied on the democratic institutions of an interventionist state to implement policies that promote social justice and cohesion within a national community. During the mid-twentieth century, this project involved establishing a compromise between the powers of capital, labour and the state to encourage the development of economic liberalization, market institutions and private property within a regulatory framework that guarantees not just the civil and political liberties of citizens, but also the social conditions necessary for people to enjoy their formal rights (Held 2004: 13). Governments performed a central role in enacting this program through the moderation of economic volatility, managing domestic demand, and providing social infrastructure, safety nets and adjustment assistance to encourage socially cohesive societies. Citizen participation in party and electoral politics ensured democratic control over the state and justified its interventions in social and economic spheres. Contemporary global forces, however, put considerable pressure on the traditional model of social democracy as the mobility of capital, goods, people, and ideas erodes the capacity of governments to sustain their own social and political compromises within delimited borders (Held 2004: 14). As Held (2004: 14) argues, globalization does not lead to the end of state choice or national political programs, but there is an increasing gap between the proclaimed values of social democracy and the regulative capacity and policy instruments available to realize them.

For cosmopolitan democrats, then, the values of social democracy – the rule of law, political equality, social justice, and social solidarity – are of enduring significance, and the key challenge today is to re-examine the conditions for their realization against a background of a changing world order. This is a particularly important task because the contemporary phase of globalization involves a shift away from exclusively state politics to multilevel forms of "global

politics" that have been shaped by interests and ideologies hostile
to social democratic values. Specifically, the neo-liberal project of
economic liberalization, privatization, and small government promoted by Western interests through global economic organizations
has contributed to the erosion of the public goods provided by the
welfare state without offering any substantial policies to deal with the
problems of market failure or increasing inequality (Held 2004: 162).
Furthermore, the US-led "war on terror" and the invasion of Iraq
in 2003 reflected a neoconservative doctrine of unilateralism that
undermines international law and the multilateral liberal order that
supported the post-Second World War welfare state (Held 2006b:
162). According to Held (2004: 162), the other prominent alternative to social democracy, radical anti-globalization, cannot offer any
solutions because it is "deeply naive about the potential for locally
based action to resolve, or engage with, the governance agenda generated by the forces of globalization." In consequence, a new project
of cosmopolitan social democracy is required that applies the values
and insights of social democracy to the new global constellation of
economics and politics.

A New Global Architecture of Cosmopolitan Democracy

For cosmopolitan democrats, the global reconfiguration of power
and authority means democracy must be institutionalized not only
at the level of the nation-state, but also at regional and global levels.
This requires a new architecture of cosmopolitan social democracy
that provides an alternative to neo-liberalism and all forms of anti-
globalization in a context where "the traditional international order
of states cannot be restored and the deep drivers of globalization
are unlikely to be halted" (Held 2004: 162). In this context, cosmopolitan democracy broadly seeks to promote the rule of law at the
international level, especially with regard to the use of force, leading
to the transcendence of the "war system" in favour of a constitutional
global order of "humane governance" (Archibugi 2008: 88–99; Falk
1995: 9; Held 1995: 279). This constitutional order would provide
greater transparency, accountability and democracy to strengthen
the principle of political equality in the management of global issues
(Archibugi 2008: 58–9, 89; Held 2004: 16–17). Furthermore, these
constitutional goals are buttressed by social democratic objectives,
which include a deeper commitment to social justice to ensure a basic
income for all adults and a more equitable distribution of life chances;

broad redistribution to alleviate the most pressing and avoidable economic harm; the reinvention of social solidarity within communities at diverse levels insofar as they depend on a set of common values and human rights; the regulation of the global economy through public management of trade and financial flows; and the engagement of leading stakeholders in corporate governance (Held 1995: 279–80; Held 2002: 36–7; Held 2004: 16–17).

Underpinning this vision is the idea that democracy ought to encompass all relationships and provide the primary grounds for institutional legitimacy at all levels and forms of government – not simply the creation of a single level of global government (Falk 1995: 254). For Daniele Archibugi (2008: 86), this rests on the conviction that democracy "is better able to satisfy the demands of the world's population than any other form of governance." But more commonly, cosmopolitan democracy is justified because it is necessary to realize *democratic autonomy* in the contemporary world. For Held (1995: 147), democratic autonomy means citizens "should be free and equal in the determination of the conditions of their own lives," so long as they do not deploy their freedoms to negate the rights of others. This requires a "common framework of political action" that specifies rights and obligations entrenched in "democratic public law," empowering and limiting individual citizens and the collective management of their affairs in a legally circumscribed structure of power (Held 1995: 143–218). This understanding of democratic autonomy involves, internally, the ability of citizens to *effectively participate* in the choices affecting their political community, and, externally, a community that is *free from domination* by others (Archibugi 2008: 88). Consequently, under conditions of contemporary globalization, democratic public law within a national political community needs to be buttressed and supported by a global structure: an overarching framework of cosmopolitan democratic law to entrench the principle of autonomy for each and every citizen, within and across every site of power (Held 1995: 207). That is, democracy must be promoted within all sites of power – local, national, transnational and international – where restrictions on political participation produce an "asymmetrical production and distribution of life chances" that limit and erode the ability of people to share in economic, cultural or political goods found in their community (Held 1995: 171). This means transferring to the global sphere democratic values such as the legal equality of citizens, the majority principle, public deliberation, and government for the common good.

The model of cosmopolitan democracy, then, is both an ideal and a program for political action that seeks to create a multi-level system of democratic governance to entrench and protect autonomy from the corrosive effects of globalization. It is an attempt to democratize the multiple and overlapping networks of power in the contemporary world through the creation of "a global and divided authority system" that incorporates local, national, regional and global layers of governance where no decision-making centre is regarded as "sovereign" in the conventional Westphalian sense of supreme and exclusive territorial authority (Archibugi 2008: 88–97; Held 1995: 234; Held 2002). The centrepiece of this system of "cosmopolitan sovereignty" (Held) or "global constitutionalism" (Archibugi) is an overarching framework of cosmopolitan law that entrenches seven principles: (1) equal worth and dignity; (2) active agency; (3) personal responsibility and accountability; (4) consent; (5) reflexive deliberation and collective decision-making through voting procedures; (6) inclusiveness and subsidiarity; and (7) avoidance of serious harm and the amelioration of urgent necessities (Held 2002: 24–32). As indicated below, vertically dispersed local, national and regional "sovereignties" are subordinated to these overarching principles of cosmopolitan law, but within this framework associations may be self-governing at diverse levels (Held 1995: 234; Pogge 1992: 58).

Crucially, the principle of inclusiveness and subsidiarity provides the fundamental basis for determining the boundaries of political constituencies. In order to ensure democratic symmetry, inclusiveness requires that those significantly affected by public decisions, issues, or processes have an equal opportunity to influence and shape them, either directly, or indirectly through elected delegates or representatives (Held 1995: 235–6; Held 2002: 28). In general, a group of individuals is considered significantly affected by a decision when it fundamentally constrains their "autonomous capacities" to shape their personal and collective lives, such as a decision leading to economic deprivation (MacDonald 2008: 40). Accordingly, subsidiarity means that democratic processes should be located at the closest level to those whose life chances are significantly affected by a policy or decision. The proper democratic constituency for addressing climate change, for example, would be global in scope, while the constituency for determining the location of a new childcare centre would be the local community that uses, operates and adjoins the centre. Carol Gould (2004: 173) has pointed out that non-territorial political communities already exist in many policy areas (constituted by those affected by the same diseases like AIDS, tuberculosis and malaria, for example). Consequently, the location of political authority in cosmopolitan democracy would be determined by the degree to which policy issues stretch across and affect populations. That is, democratic authority would be tied to the inclusion of all those affected rather than the idea of fixed sovereign borders and territories governed by states alone (Held 2002: 33). As explained below, cosmopolitan democrats do retain an important role for territorially based political communities, especially those of nation-states. However, the levels of territorial authority would owe the extent of their constitutional power to an effort to incorporate the all-affected principle (Saward 2000: 37).

The constitutional path is important to cosmopolitan democrats because the development of a unified and interconnected legal system is viewed as a fundamental step in transforming international politics from a domain of war and antagonism to one of common rights and obligations. Crucially, this constitutionalization of politics must be underpinned by a cosmopolitan *union of states* that institutionalizes global governance through a legal coding of relationships in which both individuals and governments have their own representatives in the global sphere (Archibugi 1998: 212; Archibugi 2008: 103). This goes further than a mere confederation where states retain their sovereign rights but consent to treaty-based cooperation in limited areas to promote democratic norms (along the lines of the liberal internationalism). Nor do cosmopolitan democrats propose a federation in which coercive powers are wholly transferred to a world government directly authorized and accountable to individual citizens (for this position see Marchetti 2008; Tannsjo 2008). Cosmopolitan democracy is considered an intermediate constitutional position between confederation and federation because it preserves significant features of the state system, but seeks to limit and enhance it through new centralized regional and global institutions. The aim is to develop democracy at multiple levels of governance by building on the democratic advances within states, rather than centralize coercive and fiscal powers in a global government that "would resemble Plato's government of guardians more than an authentically democratic government" (Archibugi 2008: 109).

The territorial nation-state thus remains a central facet of political organization in cosmopolitan democracy, but would acquire a transformed and somewhat diminished role in comparison with new regional and global institutions that are needed to realize cosmopolitan principles (e.g. in areas like economic and environmental regulation) (Held 2003: 35). Indeed, H. Patrick Glenn (2013) argues that the "cosmopolitan state" is already an empirical reality and the only appropriate conceptualization of the state in an era of globalization. In terms of decision-making, states would participate as equals in intergovernmental institutions according to the principle of "one government, one vote," but cosmopolitan institutions would also be created based on equality among world citizens guaranteed by the principle of "one individual, one vote" (Archibugi 2008: 104). Membership of intergovernmental organizations is regulated by the principle of effective control over territory, excluding only governments that violate fundamental human rights (Archibugi 2008: 103–4). States would accept the compulsory jurisdiction of international courts, including the International Criminal Court. Importantly, states would retain their own armed forces, but some coercive powers would shift to regional and global institutions authorized to carry out humanitarian interventions to prevent acts of genocide (Archibugi 2008: 105). Eventually, the nation-state would "wither away" in the sense that its sovereignty would be limited by global constitutional rules aimed at ensuring democratic autonomy and thus would no longer be regarded as the sole centre of political power (Archibugi 2008: 104–5; Held 1995: 233).

In addition to a cosmopolitan union of states, the crowning feature of cosmopolitan democracy is the eventual creation of a global parliament, or "Global Peoples Assembly" (GPA). For cosmopolitan democrats, a parliament that is directly elected by world citizens must be part of any serious attempt to address the global democratic deficit (Falk and Strauss 2001: 213–14). A global parliament would deal with specific *global* issues such as the environment, demographic issues, development and disarmament; or with broader political mandates such as the safeguarding of fundamental human rights and future generations, or even identifying the appropriate levels of governance for cross-border issues (Archibugi 2008: 112, 173). Most proposals envisage the electoral constituencies for a GPA as being situated in territorial states, but also see possibilities for allocating reserved seats for non-territorial communities such as the Roma, and stateless people such as the Palestinians. Johan Galtung (2000: 158) suggests that each state should have the right to one representative for every one million people (amounting to approximately 7,000 parliamentarians today), which he concedes is "unwieldy but not impossible." George Monbiot (2003: 133) argues that a parliament of 600 delegates is appropriate, but with a model of proportional representation to ensure people from smaller countries are fairly represented and to offset the excessive influence that could be wielded by countries with large populations.

Aware of the political obstacles, cosmopolitan democrats tend to propose an initially "weak" assembly constituted by existing democratic societies and aided by receptive states. This nascent parliament would have an advisory role that could begin to address these issues while posing only a long-term threat to the realities of state power (Falk and Strauss 2001: 217). It would sit alongside the UN General Assembly (representing states) and supplement rather than replace IGOs and local initiatives addressing global issues. Richard Falk and Andrew Strauss (2001: 216–17) argue that this assembly could help to promote the peaceful resolution of international conflicts; exercise democratic oversight of IGOs such as the IMF, WTO and World Bank; shape the global agenda and challenge the ability of states to opt out of collective efforts to protect the environment and control or eliminate weapons, for example; and encourage compliance with international norms and standards, especially in human rights. The significant cost of meeting facilities, translation services and other support staff for parliamentary activities could be met by contributions from supportive democratic states and international taxes on air tickets and financial transactions (Archibugi 2008: 118). Given its electoral mandate, these monitory functions would likely be followed by formal legislative powers over time as international institutions attempt to secure the approval of a democratically elected assembly (Falk and Strauss 2000: 215). If the institution were successful, people from all parts of the world, including those from nondemocratic states, would demand representation. This would give individual citizens legal rights and legislative standing in global politics.

In order for citizens to exercise these rights, however, cosmopolitan democrats argue that it is necessary to *regulate capitalism* to establish the social and economic conditions for effective participation and a fair and equal electoral system. This involves the elimination of poverty and the creation of social arrangements with the capacity to meet the basic needs of every person, including the need for self-esteem, health, a sustainable environment, and meaningful and safe work for those of this and future generations (Falk 1995: 172). Crucially, this means the legal rights and social conditions for establishing cosmopolitan democracy must be bridged by the political interventions in the global economy. For Held (1995: 266), cosmopolitan law is enhanced "through its enactment in the agencies and organizations of economic life; through democratic deliberation and coordination of public investment priorities; through the pursuit of non-market policies to aid fair outcomes in market exchange, and through experimentation with different forms of ownership and control of capital." Democratic autonomy requires that the production, distribution and allocation of resources must be focused on "transforming the conditions of those whose circumstances fall radically short of equal membership in the public realm" (Held 1995: 271). While Held (1995: 248) accepts the argument that an unbounded concept of politics can in practice lead to powerful actors controlling all aspects of life, he argues that "if the rule of law does not involve a central concern with distributional questions and matters of social justice, it cannot be adequately entrenched, and the principle of autonomy and democratic accountability cannot be realized adequately." Thus cosmopolitan democracy requires a "double-democratization": the interdependent transformation of both state and civil society (Held 2006a: 276).

These institutional innovations and redistributive goals are ultimately directed at the development of *cosmopolitan citizenship* that will allow individuals to participate in the management of global problems. The underlying assumption is that the creation of cosmopolitan institutions will produce a globally conscious citizenry: a global parliament with representatives directly elected by citizens would be more likely to promote global policies rather than state-centred ones, and will foster the sense of global community required for electoral politics and economic redistribution (Archibugi et al. 2000: 136; Archibugi 2004: 461). This is precisely the assumption that is rejected by liberal internationalists like Robert Keohane in their argument about the impossibility of a global electoral democracy (see Chapter 3). However, cosmopolitan citizenship is not intended to replace national citizenship. Rather, the development of global and transnational identities fostered by cosmopolitan institutions is the basis for a different kind of citizenship consisting of multiple and overlapping loyalties. According to Held (2000: 28), if the possibility of cosmopolitan democracy is to be consolidated:

> each citizen of a state must learn to become a cosmopolitan citizen – a person capable of mediating between national traditions, communities and alternative forms of life. Citizenship in a democratic polity of the future must increasingly involve a mediating role: a role which encompasses dialogue with the traditions and discourses of others with the aim of expanding the horizons of one's own framework of meaning and prejudice, and increasing the scope of mutual understanding. Political agents who can reason from the point of view of others are likely to be better equipped to resolve, and resolve fairly, the new and challenging transboundary issues that create overlapping communities of fate.

At the heart of cosmopolitan democracy, then, is an argument for developing cosmopolitan citizens that enjoy membership in a diverse range of political communities that significantly affect them, from the local to the global. The creation of global and transnational institutions will create cosmopolitan political horizons to inform action in the global common good. Cosmopolitan democrats contend that this is the only justifiable response to the pressing political challenges posed by globalization.

The Pathways to Cosmopolitan Democracy

Not surprisingly, such a wide-ranging and ambitious agenda for the democratization of global politics has attracted significant criticism. Within global democratic theory, the underlying aim of cosmopolitan democrats to promote democratic autonomy in an era of globalization has widespread appeal, but many democratic theorists have serious concerns about the ability of a new global architecture to generate the conditions for democratic politics beyond the nation-state. These concerns are of two kinds: concerns about the risks of shifting democracy away from the nation-state onto global and non-territorial foundations; and skepticism about the *feasibility* of creating a new cosmopolitan architecture and the absence of any systematic consideration about the political pathways for getting us there.

The first set of concerns is based on the claim that democracy has traditionally needed a territorial state to safeguard democratic institutions and guarantee citizenship rights and obligations. Michael Saward (2000: 38) argues that the protection of democratic rights requires a territorial foundation because the grounds of citizenship and rightful political participation can only be clearly defined by membership in a territorial entity. As long as membership of a permanent territorial community is in place, the all affected principle is attractive as a *supplementary guide* for democratic reform that advances the claims of groups commonly affected by cross-border issues (Saward 2000: 37–8). A baseline territorial unit is also necessary for Carol Gould (2006: 50) who argues that the democratization of global and transnational cooperative activities (perhaps using the all affected principle) hinges first on the protection of basic democratic rights within a territorial community. People cannot democratize global governance or effectively participate in global institutions if they are denied basic democratic rights in the territories where they reside and work. While supplementing them with participation rights in communities beyond the nation-state is certainly achievable (e.g. in the EU), transferring the constitutional power to enforce basic democratic rights to global institutions is an enormous and democratically risky endeavour. Furthermore, republicans and communitarians would emphasize the importance of citizenship and some sense of patriotism and public virtue as being important political preconditions for creating shared burdens and the redistribution of resources (S. Slaughter 2005: 177–9). As such, it is necessary to recognize that the starting point for pursuing cosmopolitan democracy is the existing set of territorial communities that guarantee basic democratic rights and practices.

From this angle, many scholars have criticized cosmopolitan democrats for using the all-affected principle as a *constitutional rule*. From within the liberal democratic tradition, Terry MacDonald (2008: 30) argues that creating such a "closed" and unified legal system presents serious practical difficulties when the current structure of global public power is fragmented and uneven in impact, and is not designed to serve any unifying democratic purposes. In this pluralist global order, the constitutional approach of cosmopolitan democracy seems inconsistent with the fluid and overlapping nature of affected communities. Difficulties arise when a new constituency is potentially required for every collective decision that needs to be made, and when the range and complexity of actions means it would be difficult or impossible to know who was affected (Bray 2011: 57; Gould 2006: 54). Furthermore, the principle seems to *restrict* constituencies to those who can demonstrate they are directly affected when it is often in the interests of democracy to involve a broad range of actors relevant to solving a social problem. Hans Agne (2006: 438–41) points out that democrats generally applaud the international community's support for the democratization of South Africa in the 1990s, even though affected South Africans had no direct involvement in decisions to apply diplomatic pressure and trade embargos. However, this is not to say cosmopolitan democrats ignore these difficulties. To address situations where demarcations among appropriate levels of decision-making are unclear or contested, they propose the creation of global constitutional courts, or "issue-boundary courts," to decide who counts as a stakeholder and assign appropriate competences (Held 1995: 237; Archibugi 2008: 101). The question of who appoints the judges in these cases is not clear, but is likely to be controversial given that boundary disputes are among of the most intense types of political conflict (Whelan 1983: 15). The important underlying assumption is that global conflicts of this kind can be resolved by constitutional and legal procedures rather than by force.

Furthermore, many critics suggest that this transition to cosmopolitan democracy threatens to unravel the hard-won democratic institutions of the nation-state. In the context of global capitalism, a diminished role for states has the potential to undermine governmental institutions that already exist to keep political and economic power accountable. As Richard Bellamy and R. J. Barry Jones (2000: 212) argue, "the weakening of established state-level public government could create a serious regulatory hole that might all too readily be filled, in the short and medium term at least, by undemocratic structures of private governance." Moreover, cosmopolitan citizenship requires an increased identification with global *representative* institutions that will inevitably be quite distant to most people. If the only avenue for citizens to participate in these institutions is through the election of global parliamentarians, or through membership of a select group of non-governmental organizations admitted to global institutions, then as powers shift to these institutions there is a risk that democracy will become even more elitist and make citizens feel even more alienated from politics. This is compounded by a problem of enforcement. When people must rely on global actors to enforce their new cosmopolitan rights, a disjuncture is created between the citizens who bear rights, and the parliamentarians, judges, and officials with the duty of acting on those rights in global institutions that have little coercive capacity (Chandler 2003: 341). As David Chandler (2003) argues, trading these new rights for old could create forms of dependency rather than empowerment that abrogate existing rights of democracy and self-government. In this context, it is likely that many citizens of nation-states will be unwilling to trade their concrete and protected rights in a territorial community for the much more abstract, fluid and conditional guarantees of cosmopolitan citizenship in multiple and overlapping constituencies (Bray 2011: 214).

While these critics suggest cosmopolitan democrats go too far in attempting to shift democracy away from territorial states, others argue that their proposals are too closely wedded to states and need to go further to create a global system that is genuinely democratic. From a "cosmo-federalist" position, Rafaele Marchetti (2008: 139) argues that cosmopolitan democracy fails to guarantee inclusion because it is based on an opaque and uncoordinated system of independent jurisdictions determined by an all affected principle of stakeholdership. Restricting democratic rights to those affected by an issue creates a "club model of democracy" that avoids direct exploitation, but not democratic exclusion: it does not grant political power to create public rules to *all* citizens regardless of their level of affectedness (Marchetti 2008: 140). This is a problem because the "clubs" are likely to be constituted by a limited number of self-appointed actors and the actual victims and vulnerable people would have little chance of being heard (Marchetti 2008: 139). Since states retain a large degree of national autonomy within an intergovernmental structure, and given that any additional global parliament would begin with only consultative powers, a participation deficit is identified that compromises the democratic credentials of the model of cosmopolitan democracy. Indeed, it is argued that the model unjustifiably relies on territorial communities to give effect to cosmopolitan and democratic ideals (Kuper 2004: 160–3); and views supra-state parliaments as the total extent of people's rule in global politics when the experience with elected regional parliaments has been disappointing, and global legislatures could well elicit even less popular engagement (Scholte 2014: 10). For Marchetti (2008: 139), this means cosmopolitan democracy should only be considered a transitional project on the way to the *federal* reform of IGOs. The long-term objective should be nothing less than an "all-inclusive democracy" involving a partial delegation of sovereignty to a centralized world government that has constitutionally entrenched powers of legislation, taxation, and coercive enforcement in relation to global public goods (Marchetti 2008: 149–69).

The second set of concerns relates to the feasibility of cosmopolitan democracy and the political pathways for realizing it. Feasibility concerns are especially pertinent given that the process of double-democratization of state and civil society would necessarily involve change on a scale that has historically only taken place in the wake of revolutionary upheavals (Roper 2011: 261). Sympathetic liberals tend to question the project of grand institutional design and its lack of a systematic analysis of the existing pattern of political relations that can be harnessed to achieve cosmopolitan democracy. For example, Terry MacDonald (2008: 30–2) argues that a top-down approach prioritizing a new constitutionalized framework of public power ignores the contemporary reality of global structural fragmentation where an underlying principled order of the kind cosmopolitan democrats want is lacking. MacDonald (2008: 89–92) contends that the first step should be to democratize the current pluralist structure of global power by creating channels of accountability for overlapping and non-exclusive "stakeholder communities" consisting of people affected by political decisions with institutional stability over time and who share core values of democratic autonomy. In this regard, the institutional pathway for generating a shared cosmopolitan citizenship is particularly open to question. One need only observe the European Union to see how the existence of a European Parliament does not preclude a strong nationalist mentality in European citizens, or indeed does not necessarily produce an informed and engaged "European" public. Cosmopolitan democrats have traditionally paid insufficient attention to how global and transnational democratic publics can be developed and therefore struggle to explain how cosmopolitan institutions could generate the necessary senses of community that would enable them to operate democratically. The failure to couple the cosmopolitan institutional ideal to pathways of democratization thus results in an approach that might be normatively attractive to liberals, but has limited usefulness in guiding social movements struggling for the democratization of existing global governance.

However, more strident criticisms emerge from those outside of the liberal tradition that see any attempt to tame international politics through new cosmopolitan institutions as completely at odds with the existing distribution of power and vested interests. Marxists, for example, categorically deny that any state of affairs approximating democratic autonomy can be achieved as long as capitalism exists – capitalist relations of production, distribution, and exchange are fundamentally exploitative and therefore inherently anti-democratic (Roper 2011: 261–2). Indeed, since cosmopolitan democracy would involve large-scale economic redistribution it would face intense resistance from capitalist classes and state elites who would seek to preserve their wealth and privileges. From this perspective, Brian Roper (2011: 264–5) asks: "what social and political forces are going to push through 'double democratization' against probably violent resistance of the powers that be?" Other "realist" critics argue that cosmopolitan democracy is a utopian fantasy that ignores the ways that conflict and difference shape all politics, and therefore is blind to the centralization of power required for cosmopolitan democracy to operate (see Zolo 1997). This charge often comes with an argument that cosmopolitan democracy is inherently undesirable because it would lead to a dangerous centralization of power. Geoffrey Hawthorn (2003: 20) argues that if cosmopolitan democracy "by some extraordinary transformation" were to be enacted, global institutions would need the capacity to enforce their orders through armed force against those who refused to comply (see also Zolo 1997: 153). In the contemporary age, this would mean a nuclear capability.

According to Hawthorn (2003: 20–1), this would be the "ultimate nightmare": a global system "run by factions of professionalized politicians for purposes of their own power, directing what would, in all but name, be a world state against which there would even in principle be no countervailing authority." Ultimately, it is simply not tenable to suggest that through parties of professional politicians facing each other in a global assembly that the voices of individuals could ever possibly be heard (Hawthorn 2003: 19–20).

Cosmopolitan democrats argue that they want to distribute power globally rather than centralize power in a world government (Archibugi 2008: 128–9), but the lack of attention to political pathways and agents is one area they concede has been underdeveloped. In recent years, cosmopolitan democrats have attempted to address this shortcoming. On the issue of feasibility, Daniele Archibugi (2008: 127) argues that it is incorrect to assert that the main actors in global politics are unanimously opposed to a democratic management of power: today's states express and represent a multitude of agents and interests, each of which has its own agenda and connections beyond the nation-state. Indeed, "cosmopolitan states" that champion equal treatment of citizens and aliens within their own borders are a key facet of any pathway to cosmopolitan democracy (Archibugi and Held 2011: 442; see also Glenn 2013). In addition, the agents with the greatest interest in supporting cosmopolitan democracy are: the *poor and dispossessed* who want to gain access to rights and opportunities to improve their lives; *migrants* who want rights in receiving countries and freedom of movement; *cosmopolitan groups* of intellectuals, businesspeople, activists and celebrities who already live cosmopolitan lives; *global stakeholders and global civil society* that have specific cross-border interests; *political parties* that increasingly have to deal with global issues; *trade unions and labour movements* whose mandate to guarantee adequate standards of living and social and economic rights is now situated in a global economy; and *TNCs* who require effective and accountable global governance to facilitate their business activities (Archibugi and Held 2011: 448–55). Moreover, perhaps recognizing their previous emphasis on institutional goals, Daniele Archibugi and David Held (2011: 437, 455–8) now argue that cosmopolitan democracy "is very unlikely to happen as a result of a single grand plan," but rather as a plethora of proposals and campaigns that combine top-down and bottom-up initiatives to develop global governance in a democratic direction. Against the background of almost no progress in the past two decades, cosmopolitan democrats now recognize that all forms of democratization rest on a bottom-up *struggle* of individuals to be heard and make power accountable.

Conclusion

Cosmopolitan democracy is a project that seeks to reorder global politics according to democratic rules. This is driven by a strong commitment to tame globalization so that democratic autonomy can be secured for all of humanity. In the words of David Held (2000: 237): "in a world of intensifying regional and global relations, with marked overlapping 'communities of fate,' the principle of autonomy requires entrenchment in regional and global networks as well as in national and local polities." The core elements of this project are global and transnational institutions constituted by all those affected by an issue, and a program of social policies and economic regulation to ensure that capitalism provides all individuals with the means to effectively exercise their human rights. In the next chapter, we address the approach of deliberative democracy, which tends to have less grand ambitions for the democratization of global politics. Deliberative democrats focus on the more limited but extremely important aim of increasing the deliberative capacity of existing global governance and creating new forms of deliberation that can contribute to wider democratic inclusion in the decision-making structures of global politics.

Key Readings

Archibugi, D. (2008) *The Global Commonwealth of Citizens: Toward Cosmopolitan Democracy*. Princeton University Press, Princeton and Oxford.

Falk, R. (1995) *On Humane Governance: Toward a New Global Politics*. Polity, Cambridge.

Held, D. (1995) *Democracy and the Global Order: From the Modern State to Cosmopolitan Global Governance*. Stanford University Press, Stanford.

Held, D. (2010) *Cosmopolitanism: Ideas and Realities*. Polity, Cambridge.

Marchetti, R. (2008) *Global Democracy: For and Against*. Routledge, London and New York.

5
Deliberative Democracy

While cosmopolitan democrats advocate a new constitutional framework with electoral institutions at the global level, concerns about the feasibility of this approach has led to the development of alternative theories of democratization. Foremost among these alternatives are theories of deliberative democracy arguing for global and transnational forms of democratic deliberation that do not depend upon the development of global electoral structures. Rather than reforming liberal forms of global governance to safeguard democracy at the level of the state, or creating new cosmopolitan institutions of electoral representation which operate in conjunction with global constitutional and judicial systems, the deliberative position is that we should develop inclusive deliberation across borders which inform the political decision-making of *existing* forms of global governance. This position rests on the claim that global forms of governance should be subject to public oversight and deliberation underpinned by a democratic ethic of dialogue. This argument is given weight by the observation that there are already a variety of transnational forms of activism and civil society operating within a global public sphere through which various public issues from around the world are being deliberated. As such, advocates of transnational deliberative democracy seek to develop the deliberative capacity of existing institutions and promote civic practices to enable public rule, rather than argue for new overarching systems of global representative democracy.

Deliberative democracy thus represents a range of approaches that advocate wider and more reflective public participation and deliberation in global decision-making. The position of deliberative democracy is animated by a concern that global governance and transnational civil society could be enhanced to allow effective public participation and deliberation in global politics, especially with respect to transnational problems. The central claim is that despite the rising profile of global governance and transnational civil society, formal IGOs and global governance are dominated by nation-states whose decisions reflect strategic negotiations based on national self-interest. It is thus argued that global governance is insufficiently transparent to public oversight and not sufficiently accountable to people affected by decisions originating from these forms of govern-ance. Furthermore, transnational civil society is also criticized for its unrealized potential to increase the range of perspectives and voices in global governance. This chapter examines transnational delibera-tive democracy in three steps. It first outlines the broad approach of deliberative democracy and its underlying rationale for democratic deliberation with respect to the challenges and opportunities pre-sented by contemporary global politics. The second section examines the positions developed by key scholars working within the delib-erative approach and related traditions, such as Jürgen Habermas, Philip Pettit, James Bohman, and John Dryzek. Finally, the chapter examines the practical concerns associated with creating genuine transnational deliberation and ensuring it has the capacity to influ-ence decision-making in formal international institutions.

Deliberative Democracy and Global Politics

Deliberative democracy has emerged as an influential account of democratic theory in recent decades, despite having antecedents in classical and contemporary political thought (Dryzek 2004: 145). While there are a number of different interpretations of deliberative democracy, one "common idea is that public deliberation – public reasoning about issues of shared concern – should be one of the principal ingredients of political life" (Brassett and Smith 2008: 72; Dryzek 2006, 2010). Deliberative democrats argue for the devel-opment of a political culture that enables individuals to engage in unconstrained deliberation about public life with their fellow citizens. This deliberative dialogue involves the exchange of arguments and opinions about social issues in order to reach a consensus and make collective decisions. Deliberation requires that arguments are *reflex-ive* in the sense that they reflect an awareness of the claims of others and the social context of one's actions, and can be modified through ongoing public debate and reasoning that has a consequential influ-ence on political decision-making (Dryzek 2004, 2010; Stokes 2006).

Importantly, such public involvement is advocated not only to make more effective decisions, but also to strengthen the legitimacy and justice of decision-making structures by ensuring that decisions are justified by public reasons that can be approved by all those involved. When focusing on the significance of deliberation, however, it is important to note that its value is not limited to its effects on formal decision-making structures or the aggregation of preferences in electoral democracy. The primary focus of deliberative theory is broadly on the substance and openness of public dialogue rather than specific institutions in which deliberation takes place.

Nevertheless, there is considerable debate about nature and boundaries of deliberative democracy and its relationship with other accounts of democratic and political theory. Deliberative democracy developed as an alternative to liberal democracy and its account of aggregating preferences through electoral processes, but it also intersects with various traditions including the liberalism of John Rawls and the critical theory of Jürgen Habermas (Stokes 2006: 54). While Rawls saw deliberation within existing liberal institutions of the state as important to developing "public reason," Habermas articulated a more radical view where deliberation is seen as a broader social process operating within a public sphere that is not necessarily connected to the state. For Habermas (1998: 244–5), democracy under conditions of social pluralism intrinsically involves the balancing of interests and political compromise where a commitment to fair *procedures* is required to produce rational and legitimate outcomes. In this Habermasian interpretation, *deliberative democracy has a critical impulse* that develops a broader political horizon for citizens in the sense that it "allows for the transformation of their views, their institutions and their social contexts" (Stokes 2006: 66). Furthermore, there is also a contrast that can be drawn between deliberative democracy and accounts of republicanism and participatory democracy, even though both of these traditions rely heavily upon public deliberation. Some scholars claim that the republican account of democracy presumes a conception of the public good rather than relying on public deliberation (Stokes 2006: 53–4), despite some republicans claiming public deliberation is an important part of constituting any notion of the public good (Pettit 2003). Participatory democrats claim that because deliberative democracy merely aims to increase deliberation within representative democracies, only participatory democracy can be considered a significant alternative to liberal democracy because it seeks to formally restructure democratic institutions and society so as to include every individual in deliberation and decision-making institutions (Pateman 2012). While there is no clean separation between deliberative democracy and liberal, republican and participatory accounts, the primary focus of this chapter is on the critical understanding of deliberative democracy.

As mentioned above, the critical underpinning of deliberative democracy has its roots in the work of Jürgen Habermas, which has influenced many scholars working on deliberative theory, especially James Bohman and John Dryzek. Habermas' approach to deliberation is informed by his critique of liberal aggregation and his alternative framework of "communicative action" and "discourse ethics." In the liberal tradition, democratic legitimacy springs from the private and secret votes of citizens, which are aggregated into a political will through the composition of parliamentary bodies using the majority principle. For Habermas, this means the democratic agency of citizens is limited to making decisions about electing and dismissing their leaders based on their individual interests, and without any way of reaching a mutual understanding of the common good: that is, liberal democratic processes "unfold blindly because no consciously executed collective decisions are possible over and above individual acts of choice" (Habermas 1998: 248). If we are to avoid the irrational and illegitimate outcomes often produced by this situation, deliberation, not aggregation, must be the cornerstone of democracy. Deliberation in parliamentary bodies and in informal networks of the public sphere is a mode of communicative action where rational opinion- and will-formation about problems affecting society as a whole can take place (Habermas 1998: 249). Furthermore, deliberation requires citizens to justify their decisions with public reasons that can be accepted by others, and subjects strategic behaviour like self-interested bargaining, pork-barrelling and horse trading to critical scrutiny. In order to produce genuine deliberation, discourse ethics involves the creation of an "ideal speech situation" in which everyone affected by a decision is hypothetically included in the discussion and able to speak. Political questions should be worked out in this setting without the corrupting influences of money and power so that citizens can reach a consensus through "the unforced force of the better argument" (Habermas 1996: 305). In this view, democratic legitimacy in the deliberative model hinges on the conditions of free communication and the institutional procedures for connecting public deliberation to formal decision-making.

Deliberative democracy, and its critical theory underpinnings, has been influential in scholarship that seeks to enhance public deliberation within existing global governance structures (Brassett and Smith 2008, 2010). While efforts by deliberative scholars to develop deliberation in practice aspires to include all those affected by a given decision-making process (Dryzek 2001: 651), it is argued that deliberative impulses can promote wider publicity and transparency which induces reflexivity in citizens, gives citizens considerable latitude to place issues on the agenda, and enhances their capacity to actively consider a variety of affected voices in the political process. This deliberative ethic emphasizes the inclusiveness of public participation, broadening the array of issues subject to democratic concern and ensuring that public deliberation will be a significant and systematic part of official decision-making processes (Stokes 2006: 54; Dryzek 2010). The primary concern of this literature is the lack of public participation in emerging global forms of governance. However, it should be noted that deliberative theory is also concerned with the limits of public participation evident in national politics – even within liberal representative states – and attempts to develop frameworks where public participation can be extended beyond the electoral aggregation of preferences. There are four important points of concern that deliberative democracy has with respect to global governance.

First, the deliberative approach contends that global governance is over-determined by the operation of states and the narrow national interests articulated by them. Beyond the more widespread concern of democratic deficits, deliberative scholars contend that individuals are more amenable to addressing global problems like climate change than states and critically question the political interests that operate to influence state policy (Dryzek, Bachtiger, and Milewicz 2011). Second, the deliberative approach is concerned with the lack of transparency often present in the operation of global forms of governance, arguing that the interests and discourses of powerful actors should be more open to public debate and critical scrutiny, despite the significant progress made by transnational activists in opening up global institutions. This lack of transparency means that the citizens of states that have established regional and global forms of governance find it difficult to hold them to account. Third, the accountability deficits of global governance are not limited to the citizens of member states; global governance is also not accountable to the broader publics around the world affected by the decisions made in these bodies. The exclusion of some or all of those affected by a decision is a key point of concern in deliberative theory given its focus on creating opportunities for inclusive public deliberation and removing the distortions that undermine just and well-reasoned responses to global problems. Finally, many deliberative theorists contend that deliberation can work beyond national forms of democracy and see opportunities for more deliberation in the development of global governance and the emergence of transnational civil society. In this view, NGOs and social movements can act as transnational channels of dialogue that operate within a reasonably open global public sphere with some capacity to represent interests of those not actively included in global decision-making processes (Stokes 2006: 68; see Dryzek 2006, 2011). For example, a deliberative context makes it possible to represent the interests of non-human species and future generations, and persuade others to care about and protect them (Eckersley 2011). Consequently, these forms of activity can enable forms of proxy representation within a global public sphere and create various opportunities to address global problems.

The practical responses of deliberative democrats are multifaceted because people have applied this conception of deliberation to a variety of political contexts at different scales in recent decades. In general terms, deliberative theory can be applied as an aspirational deliberative ethos that can inform and guide a system of political decision-making, even if this impulse falls short of including all those affected in decision-making processes or creating a consensus of all those involved. Beyond the promotion of a political culture of deliberation, the purpose and potential of deliberative democracy is evident in attempts to institutionalize deliberation within a broader political process. In particular, there have been attempts to experiment with deliberative mechanisms in specific sites and scales of politics around the world, including the formation of deliberative polls, citizen juries and mini-publics (Dryzek 2010: 6–9). These institutionalized forums involve small groups of citizens that are either self-selected or randomly selected from the broader population to actively engage in deliberations on specific issues in a manner often far removed from the partisan nature of electoral democracy. Some deliberative forums are designed to focus on one specific problem. Examples include the citizen juries with respect to Genetically Modified Organisms in Britain during Tony Blair's government (Goodin 2012: 807); and the 2009 World Wide Views project which organized citizen deliberation on climate change in 38 countries (Dryzek 2011: 215). Other deliberative forums are more free-ranging in terms of agenda: for example, in 2009 the Australian National University initiated an Australian Citizens' Parliament to discuss a range of issues including education and electoral systems.

Experiments with various small-scale deliberations point to a range of benefits, not the least of which is ensuring that the opinions of citizens are more thoroughly informed, even where there remain points of disagreement between the participants (Goodin 2012: 806). Yet there is still scholarly debate about how small-scale deliberations can legitimately reflect society and influence formal authority structures. As Robert Goodin (2012: 807) claims: "what right do the particular twenty people on some citizens' jury, or two hundred people involved in some deliberative poll, speak for all the rest of their fellow citizens"? There are also practical questions about how randomly selected forums of citizens relate to elected representatives or more generally to constitutional and legal structures. These questions, and other practical challenges in developing, funding and sustaining deliberative forums, suggest we must also consider how existing forms of public deliberation could be enhanced to be more transparent, reflexive and inclusive. While there are concerns that the development of small-scale forums may mean that the larger ambitions of deliberative democracy are ignored (Dryzek 2012: 6), these smaller forums point to the experimental and practical turn in deliberative democratic theory that has taken place in recent decades as well as to the latent promise of the deliberative approach.

The broader normative and aspirational impulse of deliberative democratic theory is to develop reflective forms of public deliberation which are able to inform formal decision-making. In essence, the goal is to create and develop the "capacity of deliberative systems" in the sense that the democratic system, in addition to any electoral mechanisms it may possess, ought to have "structures to accommodate deliberation" which are "authentic" (which prompt citizen reflection about political preferences and priorities), "inclusive" (include those people affected by the decision-making processes), and "consequential" (deliberation needs to be able to influence decision-making) (Dryzek 2010: 10). While many deliberative democrats aspire to develop a deliberative system within a liberal democratic state (as explained above), deliberative principles and practices can apply to a wide variety of settings without liberal institutions. The focus on deliberation broadly emphasizes the importance of civil society and the influence of social movements and NGOs within the context of a specific public sphere (Dryzek 2010: 13). As demonstrated in some of the smaller-scale forums, this means it is possible for citizens to create cross-border forms of deliberation that are able to reflect productively on complex problems with transnational impacts.

Transnational Deliberative Democracy

While the experimental edge of deliberative democracy has addressed transnational issues – as evident in the 2009 World Wide Views project – most deliberative democrats in global democratic theory have focused on the prospective role of transnational civil society and a global public sphere in developing the deliberative capacity of global governance. As indicated in the previous section and Chapter 2, existing global governance and transnational civil society have provided a context where deliberation and communication is a prominent aspect of global politics. Indeed, deliberative theory has played a prominent role in identifying the actual processes and latent possibilities for transnational activism and civil society networks to contest the decision-making of nation-states and global governance. However, while deliberative scholars generally celebrate the ways in which contemporary forms of transnational deliberation challenge the Westphalian image of state-centred global politics, they also lament the shortcomings, distortions, and deficiencies of this emerging context of political deliberation (Dryzek 2012: 216). As such, deliberative scholars seek to develop proposals that enhance existing deliberations and their influence on transnational decision-making, but also seek to develop new forms of decision-making that are better able to promote inclusion, legitimacy, and justice in the effective management of transnational problems.

Despite agreement on these general goals, deliberative theorists differ with regard to how deliberation ought to operate within global politics. First, there are important differences concerning why and how deliberation is valuable, with some scholars seeing deliberation as intrinsically valuable for its necessary role in constituting global justice, while others see deliberation as instrumentally useful in addressing complicated collective problems by developing new ideas and sources of information to challenge existing forms of knowledge and authority (Bohman 2007: 173–4, Dryzek 2011: 213–14). Second, deliberative theorists also differ with regards to how strongly deliberation can and should be politically institutionalized. Dryzek (2011: 211) articulates the breadth of possibilities by referring to the existence of "soup" of ad hoc forms of democratic practice, a "society" of democratic practices being underpinned by common norms, and "system" where democratic practices are formally developed and maintained. Third, due to this breath of possibilities, there are differences in emphasis concerning where deliberation ought to be located. Some scholars seek to foster a deliberative culture or system at a global level, while others seek to locate deliberation within existing forms of global governance or within specific IGOs. As such, there are a variety of scholarly responses to how deliberation can be institutionalized in global politics.

The first main response focuses upon the deliberative capacity and potential of existing forms of global governance. The critical theory underpinnings of deliberative theory is evident here because these scholars want to work with the institutions "we have" in order to identify possible pathways of transforming them into more inclusive deliberative contexts, rather than arguing for grand systems of global electoral democracy (Brassett and Smith 2008: 84). There have been various efforts to deploy deliberative impulses in specific forms of global governance including developing principles that inform international law (Goodin and Ratner 2011), international financial governance (Germain 2010), the WTO (Higgott and Erman 2010), and the G20 (S. Slaughter 2013). These theoretical engagements with existing global governance have generally demonstrated how these forums involve extensive forms of dialogue, but that they fall significantly short of satisfying the deliberative ideal of including citizens in a systematic fashion or facilitating authentic, inclusive and consequential forms of deliberation. In general, the deliberation in these institutions does not give adequate weight to those most significantly affected by their decision-making processes, especially people in disadvantaged states, and gives too much influence to voices of powerful states and market actors. Yet there is an argument that through the ongoing engagement of transnational activism this situation may be open to change. The forums of global governance could act as what Randall Germain (2010: 501) terms an "institutional anchor," which creates public spheres constituted by deliberation between officials of global governance and the publics in member states, the publics of states that are not members, and transnational civil society. The potential to create meaningful forms of dialogue and accountability is one that these deliberative scholars attempt to realize in specific contexts of global governance.

A second response is evident in the neo-roman republicanism of Philip Pettit. This position articulates a practical and institutional conception of republicanism that shares some features with liberal internationalism, but also overlaps with deliberative theory. Pettit (1999a: 152) has a clear focus on the necessity of a democratic state, informed by constitutionalism and shaped by virtuous citizens to achieve the republican aspiration to promote liberty. But he also recognizes the importance of deliberation between states to create forms of international law able to "establish a culture" to minimize domination (Pettit 2010: 83). Pettit (2003) also illuminates the connections between republicanism and deliberative democracy by identifying the importance of citizens having avenues to challenge decision-making processes. He advances the idea of "contestatory democracy" where citizens of a republican state have both "authorial" and "editorial" capacities in relation to government (Pettit 1999b: 180). Authorial power encompasses the democratic selection of representatives, while editorial power includes democratic measures that maximize the presence of minority voices, promote dialogue, and keep the actions of government transparent and accountable in order to promote public interests. Pettit (2005: 14–15) claims that if we conceive of democracy in contestatory terms we can identify avenues which extend the opportunities for citizens to hold governments to account. Not only could principles of deliberation and contestation be extended to government policies within global governance, but contestatory democracy opens up the possibility that citizens could appeal to IGOs or transnational NGOs when state leaders fail to uphold their declared obligations (Pettit 2005: 16–20). As such, this response sees no inherent contradiction between a political community existing at a national level and transnational forms of deliberation.

A third and more wide-ranging response is evident in the work of Jürgen Habermas and James Bohman and their ambitious efforts to theorize more deliberative and inclusive political communities beyond the nation-state. For Habermas (2001: 62–80), trends toward a "postnational constellation" are evident as globalization erodes the basic functions and legitimacy of democratic nation-states. Crucially, as the national basis for solidarity weakens, he believes that a "constitutional patriotism" based on specific and legally constructed interpretations of popular sovereignty and human rights can take the place of nationalism in binding together a democratic community (Habermas 1999: 118–19). This kind of civic solidarity can be extended to postnational federations like the EU in order to create constitutional structures supporting a rights-based collective identity, a supranational parliament, a functioning party system and a transnational public sphere. But that is as far as postnational democracy can go. Global democracy is not possible because "even a worldwide consensus on human rights could not serve as the basis for a strong equivalent to the civic solidarity that emerged in the framework of the nation-state" (Habermas 2001: 108). Indeed, the cosmopolitan solidarity that underpins models of cosmopolitan democracy (see

Chapter 4) must rest on the moral universalism of human rights and therefore lacks the common ethical and political culture that would be necessary for a global democratic community (Habermas 2001: 108). Consequently, Habermas sees postnational democracy, as evident in the EU, as an order underpinned by international human rights law and a political culture based on commitments to these rights, to constitutionally entrenched democratic processes, and to civil society deliberations in transnational public spheres.

Bohman (2007) develops a similar argument about the effect of globalization on the nation-state, but he sees Habermas as being too limited in terms of the substance and limits of transnational deliberation: it should not just include consideration of transnational problems but also the nature and boundaries of the political community itself. Bohman's conceptualization of deliberative democracy focuses upon achieving the republican goal of non-domination. He starts with the observation, which concurs with Habermas, that political theory must move beyond the state to address international and transnational forms of domination (Bohman (2007, 2008: 192–3). As such, he claims that a synthesis of republican, cosmopolitan and pragmatic strands is necessary to rethink the nature of political deliberation and obligation. Bohman (2008: 197, 2007: 55) claims that non-domination needs to be delinked from a republican conception of the state and instead citizens need to have an active capacity to "create and modify their own obligations and duties" rather than them being assumed and imposed from the republican state. He thus offers an ideal of "transnational republicanism" which outlines the basic conditions of global democratization and aims to realize a "democracy of *dêmoi*" (Bohman 2007). This involves abandoning ideals that demand a social limitation of the community and a central authority controlled by a singular, self-legislating *demos*. Bohman (2007: 45ff) sees the basis of democratic reconstruction as grounded in a "democratic minimum": a fundamental power to initiate deliberation across borders that accrues to all people as citizens of a transnational human political community.

Bohman is opposed to the idea that *dêmoi* should be subsumed into a cosmopolitan hierarchy of sovereignty with a global *demos* at its apex; or an understanding of non-domination that simply involves a power to contest decisions evident in Pettit's conception of contestatory democracy. The capacity to begin deliberation about transnational injustices "provides the basic measure for the status of person required for democratization" and involves converting contestatory claims into effective political power (Bohman 2007:

53). Non-domination thus requires a form of popular control that involves the exercise of fundamental citizenship powers in a variety of overlapping *dêmoi*, some of which may be global in scope and involve a greater awareness of humanity as a form of "transnational political community" (Bohman 2008: 192). If this is to be realized, current boundaries and membership must be included in the open agenda of deliberation because "democracy is that set of institutions and proce-dures by which individuals are empowered as free and equal citizens to form and change the conditions of their common life together, including democracy itself" (Bohman 2007: 45). This is an intrinsic defence of the significance of transnational forms of deliberation and democracy (Bohman 2007: 173), and significant departure from the republican focus on the state or a cosmopolitan focus on an electoral conception of cosmopolitan democracy.

Finally, a fourth response is evident in John Dryzek's arguments for enhancing the deliberative potential and capacity of transnational civil society. Dryzek (2001, 2006) is quick to emphasize that delib-erative democracy does not require global electoral mechanisms. This indicates an acceptance of the unstructured and decentralized nature of the debates within transnational civil society, but this approach seeks to infuse a reflexive deliberative culture into the activity of agents operating within this context, thereby nurturing a diverse array of political perspectives (Dryzek 2006, 2012). The primary virtue of agents within transnational civil society is that they authentically represent certain ideas, values, and discourses which may be marginalized or not actively considered by government nego-tiations in global politics. Despite not being elected by anyone, trans-national activists and NGOs can act as representers of discourses and therefore enhance democracy by widening the perspectives bearing upon political decision-making. With reference to such activists and NGOs, Dryzek and Simon Niemeyer (2008: 491) inquire:

> Is the world any more democratic for their activities? Clearly, yes, the international governmental institutions they target now have to justify their activities in light of a variety of discourses, whereas previously they either felt no need to justify at all, or did so in narrowly economistic and administrative terms. Thus, the idea of discursive representation provides democratic validation for the activities of NGOs and other transnational activists.

This representative role could be enhanced in a number of ways. One approach that stems from the experimental strand of delib-erative theory mentioned earlier is based on a proposal to create a global deliberative forum referred to as a "Deliberative Global Citizens' Assembly" (DGCA) (Dryzek et al. 2011). In contrast to the cosmopolitan desire for an elected forum (see Chapter 4), the DGCA would be a semi-randomly selected body of individuals based upon some stratification to equally represent the world's population, which could act as an advisory body to deliberate specific issues. By being separate from any formal authority, it would mean that citizens would not be representatives of their states and thus free to deliberate without reference to national interests. Consequently, the DGCA could act as "focal point for the development of global deliberative systems spanning the public space of global civil society and the empowered space of public authority" (Dryzek, Bachtiger, and Milewicz 2011: 40).

Dryzek has also advanced a variant of deliberative democracy called "discursive democracy" which seeks to develop the communicative power of transnational civil society and its reflexive control of discourses. This approach to transnational democracy aims to democratize the discursive sources of governance that are already present in the international system, rather than to introduce new system-level democratic institutions. Dryzek (1999) argues that in a context of weak formal rules in international politics, discourses play a much greater role in coordinating action than in domestic society. It is therefore important what balance of discourses holds sway in the international system. His core claim is that "this balance or interplay can be brought under conscious, collective, and ultimately democratic control" (Dryzek 1999: 37). Democracy in this context refers to a situation where there is the "dispersed and competent control over the collectively consequential engagement of discourses in the global public sphere" (Dryzek 2012: 115). This means that the scope of democracy must be extended beyond the nation-state by subjecting existing discourses to broad deliberative contestation that can challenge global institutional agendas and unaccountable sites of transnational power, and empower progressive forces of transnational civil society. He cites discursive contests in areas like ozone depletion, whaling, "bioprospecting," and sustainable development as examples where broad contestation in transnational issue communities led to important political outcomes, some of which involved securing environmental protections in opposition to powerful state actors (Dryzek 1999: 39–43). The democratic potential of a reflexive civil society is therefore the key element in challenging forms of unjustified exclusion and building a more equal and environmentally sustainable world.

Crucially, this understanding of transnational democracy involves the representation of discourses rather than individuals. Indeed, Dryzek argues that it is possible and far easier for civil society groups to represent discourses rather than the interests of specific individuals in global politics; where discourses are understood as identifiable narratives which enable individuals to create "coherent accounts organized around storylines that can be shared in intersubjectively meaningful ways" such as market liberalism, human rights and sustainable development (Dryzek 2006: 1–2). Although there are practical questions concerning who represents discourses, how these representers are selected, and how these representations should inform policy-making (Dryzek and Niemeyer 2008), this form of democracy is explicitly targeted at enhancing deliberation at the global level. While this discursive representation does not necessarily require formal institutionalization, Dryzek and Niemeyer (2008) have proposed the creation of a "chamber of discourses" that would include self-selected or randomly selected individuals operating as a "mini-public" that could operate alongside electoral forums. A chamber of discourses could provide a deliberative forum when the inclusion of all-affected is unfeasible, especially in transnational settings lacking a well-defined *demos*. Moreover, it could "provide a check on the degree to which the formal chamber features a comprehensive and accurate set of the relevant discourses, and promote discursive accountability by calling changes of language in the formal chamber to account" (Dryzek and Niemeyer 2008: 491). Such a chamber could operate alongside the UN, for example, and provide a forum that could help achieve inclusive and reflective deliberation on transnational issues.

Criticisms of Transnational Deliberative Democracy

The central point of contention between these various accounts of deliberative democracy is the question of how deliberation can best be facilitated and institutionalized. There is widespread agreement among these scholars that the political activity of transnational civil society could play a significant role in enhancing deliberation in global politics and improving the effectiveness and legitimacy of global governance. The general contention is that reflexive deliberation produces mutual forms of recognition, engagement and learning which can lead to better decision-making and more effective policies for those affected. This approach recognizes the forms of deliberation emerging between global governance and transnational civil society, but argues that these forms of dialogue need to be rethought in accordance with the maxims and principles of deliberative theory to create new institutions and modes of transnational deliberation. Within the broader context of global democratic theory, it is clear that the transnational account of deliberative democracy has strengths which derive from its practical approach. In terms of feasibility, it sees no need to centralize power and law at the global level or create formal institutions which challenge state sovereignty and generate complex political mechanisms of a world government. The deliberative account attempts to work with the existing forms of global governance and transnational civil society. Moreover, the value of inclusive and reflective communication has been demonstrated in practical experiments of deliberative democracy – it is not merely a figment of speculative theoretical reflection.

However, there are still serious difficulties in identifying precisely how these various deliberative measures can influence formal authorities in global politics, as well as concerns about what sorts of skills and dispositions citizens need to make deliberation work in transnational contexts. That is, the critical question concerning the deliberative approach is to what extent can meaningful transnational deliberation be realized in order to influence sites of international authority? Naturally, any answer to this question rests on the standard of assessment levied upon transnational deliberation. The highest standard for deliberation is encapsulated in the maxim that "outcomes are legitimate to the extent they receive reflective assent through participation in authentic deliberation by all those subject to the decision in question" (Dryzek 2001: 651); whereas a more modest standard would assess whether a system of governance is more responsive and accountable to people subject to it because of improved forms of deliberation. As indicated above, the practical intent of deliberative theory means that this more modest standard, which falls short of the all-inclusive aspiration, is still valuable yardstick for judging transnational deliberation. There are three lines of critique about the capacity of deliberative democracy to realize either of these standards in contemporary global politics.

The first line of critique facing the deliberative approach focuses upon the limits of emerging forms of transnational deliberation. From a practical perspective, not everyone around the world can be included in global decision-making so questions remain about whether NGOs and civil society organizations are a reasonable proxy and whether a global public sphere is the appropriate setting for deliberative democracy. There are a range of concerns about the deliberative role of transnational actors given that some CSOs and NGOs do not have high levels of internal or external accountability. These organizations may also have strategic and financial imperatives that shape what they do which may differ from the people they purport to serve, thereby distorting their deliberative capacity (Bob 2002). It is also the case that a digital divide persists in global politics which means Western NGOs tend to dominate civil society participation and other organizations representing the poor and marginalized may not have enough resources to be able to act independently or effectively convey their message in global policy-making. Furthermore, many CSOs are not progressive or democratic in outlook and actually directly or indirectly engage in dialogue that either reinforces the status quo or actively opposes democracy (see Chambers and Kopstein 2001). For example, pro-capitalist think tanks have played a highly influential role in debates about the nature of global economic rules, and the USA's National Rifle Association has sought to derail negotiations on the regulation of the small arms in the UN. As such, there are serious questions about whether transnational actors and global governance systems can create the types of dialogue needed to facilitate deliberation and the representation of various marginalized interests.

Deliberative democrats are aware of these limits to deliberation and the problems of representation associated with transnational actors. Dryzek (2012: 107), for example, argues that when confronted by criticisms about whether global civil society actually enables reflective deliberation or is substantively unrepresentative:

> A better response to the charge is to ask: Unrepresentative compared to what? Compared to some ideal model of egalitarian democracy, global civil society may do badly. Compared to other realities in a global order dominated by large corporations, hegemonic states, neoliberal market thinking, secretive and unresponsive international organizations, low-visibility financial networks, and military might, global civil society does rather well.

Dryzek indicates that the key issue is whether this transnational activity has made global politics more transparent and democratic in the sense of "expanding the scope of issues subject to collective control, the effective number of people who can exercise influence over the content of collective decisions, and the competence with which such influence and control is exercised" (Dryzek 2012: 107). In this regard, while it is necessary to be aware of the limits and distortions within global civil society, it is also important to recognize the opportunities for public participation in a domain which has traditionally been opaque and unreceptive to public involvement in decision-making.

A second line of critique relates to a more specific problem concerning the possibility of creating consensus in global politics. While a global civil society and a global public sphere offer increased opportunities for public deliberation, the sheer variety of voices and interests makes arriving at a consensus position on a given issue extremely difficult, in which case civil society is limited to merely contesting decision-making. Indeed, while deliberative democracy does not demand a complete consensus for political action, it has long been criticized for being overly idealistic about the prospects for consensus at a meta-level where some agreement is required on the structures that frame deliberation, as well as the prospects of subsequent deliberation being rendered into a workable consensus for political action. Scholars from the account of "agonistic pluralism" within democratic theory have contended that conflict and ineradicable differences of perspective are key features of modern democracy that the "consensus approach" of deliberative theorists largely evades (Mouffe 1999). For Chantal Mouffe (1999: 753, 2000: 101–5), the impossibility of evading pluralism and conflict means politics must "constitute forms of power that are compatible with democratic values" by transforming hostile antagonisms between enemies into agonistic struggles between adversaries who combat ideas but do not question each other's right to defend those ideas. The consequences of pluralism and the inevitability of conflict take on an even more dramatic nature within global politics with its wider diversity of cultural and political values. From an agonistic perspective, a rational consensus is impossible in global politics and civil society activity will be limited to contesting the ideas and decision-making of hegemonic groups (Mouffe 2011). These problems are accompanied by a lack of clarity in many accounts of deliberative democracy regarding how transnational deliberation should interface with states and how conflicts should be resolved between transnational deliberations led by NGOs and domestic political outcomes and processes.

Deliberative scholars have different views with respect to these criticisms. In terms of consensus, there is a general view that the overarching objective of transnational deliberation is to broaden political horizons and break down any clear distinction between national and global politics where any consensus achieved is simply a contingent moment subject to ongoing debate. Some deliberative scholars such as Pettit and Habermas point to the importance of the state as a site of policy creation that can be actively informed by transnational deliberation. As indicated above, Bohman (2010: 4) argues that the more fundamental objective for transnational deliberation is to form and change a common democratic life that goes beyond "contestation" to encompass "the capability of citizens to transform communicative freedom into communicative power" that recognizes and includes all persons and does not privilege arbitrary state boundaries. Dryzek avoids directly focusing upon the state or transforming political community and contends that transnational activity does have a discursive impact which goes beyond contestation and does not require formal institutional linkages to the state or any other site of formal authority. Challenging dominant discourses and representing alternatives is a key aspect of transnational deliberation that can foster political change. The role of civil society in representing discourses in deliberative settings is emphasized because civil society actors have greater capacity to act reflectively than states because states are "heavily constrained by their imperatives to ensure their own security, maintain legitimacy in the eyes of their own populations, and maximize economic growth" (Dryzek 2012: 115). This means that civil society deliberations produce a much wider horizon of imagination and political action (Brassett and Smith 2010). Again, these positions differ with regards to how deliberation can be institutionalized and whether universal inclusion of every person is possible, but there is an underlying confidence that the contestatory role of transnational civil society does not rule out various other creative possibilities.

The final line of critique of the deliberative approach relates to the possibility of developing the political dispositions and skills of citizens required for transnational deliberation to work. While civil society deliberation may indeed foster greater diversity, reflexivity, and imagination than interstate negotiations, there are questions about whether citizens have the political skills, education, and leadership qualities to deliberate on transnational issues in a sustained fashion. Some form of cosmopolitan sensibility is seemingly required to take a global view and take the views, interests, or suffering of distant others seriously. Furthermore, engaging in genuine transnational deliberation requires one to be conscious of the corrupting and distorting power of vested interests. While Pettit advances the republican claim that citizen virtue is required to create these qualities, Habermas and Bohman are less forthcoming about the personal political dispositions that must underpin transnational deliberation and enable the transformation of political community they seek. In this regard, it is doubtful that a patriotic commitment to constitutional rules is enough to sustain authentic transnational deliberation. Recognizing this deficiency, Dryzek has pointed out that deliberative scholars are actively examining the dispositions of people participating in mini-public types of deliberative forums, and that given the chance people engage reflectively and enthusiastically. He also argues that the mass societal involvement of virtuous citizens is not required to enhance transnational deliberations because this can be done through small-scale deliberative mechanisms such as the DGCA (Dryzek, Bachtiger, and Milewicz 2011: 40). The important point for Dryzek is that democratic deliberation requires the nurturing of a public sphere where all discourses relevant to an issue are represented in order for power to be more transparent. When powerful discourses like market liberalism must engage with other discourses of human rights and sustainable development, for example, debates about social problems become more open and inclusive and foster decisions that are supported by public reasons rather than strategic interests.

Conclusion

While debates will continue about the merits and deficiencies, desirability and feasibility of the deliberative approach, it is clear that the development of transnational civil society provides an important and intriguing context for this form of global democratic theory. As this chapter has demonstrated, it is also clear that deliberative theorists and scholars working within related political traditions have developed a range of normative models that point to a wide variety of practical innovations and political possibilities. Whether the goal is universal deliberation that includes all those affected, or a more modest aim to increase the deliberative capacity and discursive accountability of a specific governance mechanism, the question of how to institutionalize and systematize the deliberative impulse is a pressing question with important political implications for the democratization of global governance. In the next chapter, we turn to the social democratic strand of global democratic theory, which emphasizes issues of political economy and advances a more direct argument about how globalization ought to be reformed or restructured.

Key Readings

Brassett, J. and Smith, W. (2008) Deliberation and global governance: liberal, cosmopolitan and critical perspectives. *Ethics and International Affairs*, 22 (1), 69–92.

Bohman, J. (2007) *Democracy across Borders: From Dêmos to Dêmoi*. MIT Press, Cambridge.

Dryzek, J. (2006) *Deliberative Global Politics: Discourse and Democracy in a Divided World*. Polity, Cambridge

Habermas, J. (2001) *The Postnational Constellation*. Polity, Cambridge.

Pettit, P. (2010) Republican law of peoples. *European Journal of Political Theory* 9 (1), 70–94.

6

Social Democracy

Social democracy in its broadest sense is a position that seeks to transform society in an egalitarian direction via regulatory policies directed by the democratic processes of the state. However, there has been an array of different positions across the history of social democratic thought, which vary between reformist efforts to moderate capitalism and more radical efforts to transform society in a socialist direction. Social democratic thought has also been paralleled by other radical positions, such as anarchism, throughout its history. The impact of globalization, and especially neo-liberalism, has drawn both radical and reformist strands into debates about how democracy ought to be configured to respond to globalization. In particular, the idea of the Third Way rose in prominence in leftist parties around the world during the 1990s as an attempt to create a viable alternative to neo-liberalism and statist social democracy. This led to criticisms from more radical scholars that this approach was too accommodating to global capitalism and strayed too far from socialist principles and priorities. While social democracy is animated by a democratic ethic of equality, there are also significant debates concerning how such arguments for promoting substantive equality relate to other approaches of democratic theory. Social democratic impulses overlap with liberal, republican and cosmopolitan thought, for example. It is also the case that social democracy intersects with deliberative democracy, but social democrats generally question the possibility of such deliberation being genuine within the context of unfettered capitalism.

This chapter is focused on the scholarly dimension of social democratic thought but is cognisant that social democracy is a broad domain which has involved numerous attempts around the world to develop these principles into political practice and public policy. These attempts include efforts from political parties, trade unions, international movements associated with socialist thought since the First International in 1864, as well as scholarly arguments from an array of reformist and radical positions. Furthermore, it is difficult to separate reformist social democratic thought from social liberalism. Nevertheless, the general position that regulation directed by the state can promote equality is an important argument with respect to how democratic thought can respond to globalization. This chapter will first outline the principles of social democracy and consider the way in which capitalist logics of contemporary globalization have challenged these democratic principles. Second, the chapter will outline the main positions of social democratic thought by examining the reformist approach of the Third Way, more substantially reformist accounts evident in work of Will Hutton and Colin Crouch, and other more radical socialist positions exemplified in the work of Alex Callinicos. Third, the chapter considers the questions surrounding the feasibility of implementing social democratic thought as a response to contemporary globalization by considering how it addresses the possibilities of democratic leadership, how social democracy ought to relate to other political traditions sympathetic with efforts to regulate capitalism, and the overall plausibility of social democratic forms of political community.

The Social Democratic Imperative

Social democracy is an approach that seeks to transform society either by moderating the worst excesses of capitalism or by transcending capitalism and developing a form of democratic planning for economic activity. Importantly, this form of political thought has been evident in the development of actual policies and institutions which seek to promote egalitarianism and human welfare in practice, especially the development of the European welfare state in the late nineteenth century and the twentieth century. Social democratic thought makes an important contribution to contemporary democratic scholarship by acting as a stark reminder that free markets are not the only way to organize economic activity. Indeed, Tony Judt (2009) makes this clear when he emphasizes the importance of remembering the legacy of social democracy with respect to the impact of unfettered capitalism:

> If social democracy has a future, it will be as a social democracy of fear. Rather than seeking to restore a language of optimistic progress, we should begin by reacquainting ourselves with the recent past. The first task of radical dissenters today is to remind their audience of the achievements of the twentieth century, along with the likely consequences of our heedless rush to dismantle them.

Fear in this context entails remembering the past horrors and dangers of unfettered capitalism and the weakening of past social democratic measures to address these aspects of capitalism. Social democracy is thus not an abstract position with respect to democratic theory and globalization, as it has a longstanding opposition to the actual dangers of unfettered capitalism, and in its past has promoted concrete ways of organizing social and economic life. However, the development of welfare state mechanisms and forms of economic regulation and redistribution in many countries have been challenged by neo-liberal processes of economic deregulation and liberalization. The question is whether social democracy as body of thought can effectively respond to the rise of contemporary globalization and neo-liberalism.

Clearly the historical legacy of social democracy needs to be seen against the broader spectrum of social democratic thought. Social democratic thought is unified by the desire to promote egalitarianism, social justice, solidarity, and the welfare of the working class, but differences exist concerning whether this goal requires the reform and moderation of capitalism or a radical revolution replacing capitalism and the development of socialist democratic planning to organize economic life. With respect to the rising impact of globalization and neo-liberalism, we have seen both reformism in Third Way governments and its attendant scholarship, as well as radicalism in elements of the anti-capitalism movement and Marxist scholarship. While some reformist accounts of social democracy were very much part of the prevailing influence of social democracy in Europe and elsewhere from the late nineteenth century, more radical accounts seeking the transcendence of capitalism were not as influential in terms of policy-making but clearly present in intellectual and political terms. Indeed, the rise of neo-liberalism and erosion of the gains made by social democracy point to the fact that the development of the welfare state – which certainly improved the lives of those in the working class – was only a temporary accommodation by capitalism not a more permanent accomplishment (Callinicos 2003: 121). This observation indicates that there is a more radical social democratic position that seeks to articulate the interests of the working class by promoting revolutions able to transcend capitalism in the sense indicated by Marxist thought. This radical account sees the transcendence of capitalism as the only way to sustain and broaden the kinds of gains created by the welfare state.

While the delineation between reformism and radicalism is the main fault line within social democratic thought, there are other points of difference. First, there is a difference between accounts of social democratic thought which possess a socialist tradition distinct from other accounts of political theory, versus accounts which are open and connected to other theories such as republicanism, anarchism and Green theory (Crouch 2013: 1, Callinicos 2003: ch. 2). While these latter accounts agree with regulating and perhaps transcending capitalism, they do not have socialist intellectual foundations and have social bases not drawn from traditional conceptions of the working class. Second, there is a point of debate in social democratic thought between advocates of elite led and mass movement strategies for the implementation of social democratic agenda. While groups like unions have played an important role in developing and enacting social democratic ideas in the policy of states, the role of the working class as a mass political force is an important issue in both reformist and radical social democracy (Crouch 2013: 2). Lastly, there is some debate in social democratic thought between the national and international articulation of social democratic ideas. While social democracy has been an international movement since its inception in the mid-1800s and is influenced by Marx's understanding of capitalism as being inherently global, the primary location of the implementation of social democratic practice has been the nation-state (Crouch 2013: 2; Held 2004: 16–17). While there are cosmopolitan accounts of social democracy, and the operation of the Socialist International association of leftist political parties and radical elements of the anti-capitalism movement is inherently international, the state looms as the key site for implementing efforts to confront and moderate capitalism.

The problem globalization and neo-liberalism poses for social democratic thought is straightforward: it is opposed to the power of unfettered capitalism and the consequences of society being determined primarily by capitalist dynamics of profitability. As such, the rise of neo-liberalism since the 1980s has directly challenged social democratic principles. The concerns of social democrats about globalization relate to both the social effects of unfettered capitalism as well as the political dynamics that stem from the increased mobility of capital enabled by neo-liberal reforms. With regard to the economic effects of globalization, it is clear that social democrats are concerned about the ways in which free market policies have entrenched inequality, poverty and social exclusion of some groups and societies around the world, as well as led to rising levels of environmental degradation (Gill 2012: 1–2; Callinicos 2003: ch. 1). In particular, the period since the 1980s has seen a marked increase in various forms of inequality across much of the developed world and developing worlds (Callinicos 2003: 22–4; Stiglitz 2002: ch. 1, 2012). This is a consequence of neo-liberal efforts to wind back the welfare state, involving cut backs in the provision of social welfare, health, and public expenditures. It is also due to the increased mobility and flexibility of transnational capital compared with the immobility of wage earning labour, which has weakened the position of organized labour in a context where firms play workplaces off against each other (Crouch 2013: 4–5). While defenders of neo-liberalism champion the idea that free markets promote innovation and economic growth, socialists and social democrats are quick to claim that economic growth since the 1980s is less impressive than the post-war period when social democracy was more influential, as well as less equally distributed (Callinicos 2003: 23). The combined effects of these developments have been decreases in personal liberty and security for many people.

Another source of considerable insecurity stems from the financialization of global capitalism involving the volatility of financial markets and the rising power and mobility of capital. The widespread deregulation of financial markets has meant that capital moves across borders more readily and affects societies more widely. Within the context of economic globalization, these crises have occurred with greater frequency and the "harms have extended far beyond the investors who knowingly take risks. Indeed, the greatest pains of global financial instability have often hit highly vulnerable social circles" (Scholte 2000: 218). Regional financial crises during the 1990s and the 2008 global financial crisis are examples of the global financial system creating significant levels of economic distress in the form of unemployment and bankruptcies. The human impact of these crises persists long after the economic problems are addressed. The subsequent interventions of international agencies like the IMF in the form of various forms of austerity, which are designed to alleviate economic instability, often have the effect of magnifying the social distress (Stiglitz 2002: ch. 1). Consequently, the global economic system can capriciously reduce and condition the social opportunities of people around the globe. This can be seen in the aftermath of the global financial crisis and the sovereign debt crisis in Europe beginning in 2009 involving attempts to impose austerity on highly indebted societies, especially Greece.

In this context, global markets frame economic decisions and this has problematic implications for the practice of democracy. Because decision-making is being conducted in global markets and global governance, the role of the liberal democratic state is unclear because various areas of public policy have been established within global governance and thus designed and enacted without active public involvement. This means public policy takes on a business-friendly cast which resists efforts to regulate or redistribute economic activity, thus making efforts to address environmental degradation and inequality unlikely to succeed. As such, the influence and power of contemporary forms of neo-liberalism is manifest in the existence of a "post democratic" context where liberal representative democracy is little more than a "tightly controlled spectacle" (Crouch 2004: 4); a charade masking technocratic and market decision-making of business interests. Nevertheless, social democratic parties still attempt to operate within liberal democratic systems around the world. Social democrats also have even deeper concerns about the ways in which the social effects of inequality and exclusion have a significant impact on the practice of democracy by sidelining underprivileged groups of society and thus privileging the interests of wealthy classes. Radical accounts of social democracy see genuine democracy as requiring substantive equality and participation, leading to doubts as to whether democracy is actually possible within capitalism. These intellectuals and activists thus champion participatory democracy and the overall goal of enabling the democratic planning of economic decision-making. The radical account is also more liable to see the ways in which dominant countries are engaged with imperialist dynamics of military competition and warfare (Callinicos 2003).

Consequently, there is little doubt that social democracy has been profoundly challenged by the significant social and political impacts of neo-liberalism, which have undermined the achievements of previous generations of social democrats. Not only have some traditional leftist parties been sidelined and disorientated by the rise of neo-liberalism, but some have played a role in developing and enacting versions of neo-liberalism. For instance, Australian and New Zealand governments in the 1980s and 1990s articulated processes of deregulation and liberalization that opened up their societies to the dynamics of global markets. This has entrenched the idea, popularized by the Conservative UK Prime Minister Margaret Thatcher, that "there is no alternative" to free markets as the most effective pathway to economic prosperity. Furthermore, there is the more general claim that since the collapse of the Soviet Union, socialism has no robust credibility to guide political life. In this context, social democratic scholarship challenges the contention that there is no alternative to liberalism and free markets. Social democrats are united in their view that the state must democratically intervene in global economy. Such a position does encompass some avowed social democratic scholars such as Anthony Giddens who claim that socialism is indeed obsolete and needs to be reconfigured, and others such as Alex Callinicos who claim that democratically guided socialism is a strong basis for an alternative program of action to that of liberals and neo-liberals. The normative claims of social democracy thus centre on how and to what extent states can wrest control over global capitalism.

The International Dimension of Social Democracy

Social democratic responses to contemporary globalization begin with the controversial and contested efforts during the 1990s and early 2000s to develop a "Third Way" between conventional accounts of social democracy and neo-liberalism. Anthony Giddens was a high profile supporter of New Labour in Britain and contended that the Third Way is

> a framework of thinking and policy-making that seeks to adapt social democracy to a world which has changed fundamentally over the past two or three decades. It is a third way in the sense that it is an attempt to transcend both old style social democracy and neo-liberalism. (Giddens 1998: 26)

At the heart of this reformulation was the idea the governments need to invest in their populations in order to enable workforces to promote social solidarity, to compete in the global economy and attract well-paying jobs (Reich 1991; Giddens 1998). This approach seeks to balance economic competitiveness within the global economy with social cohesion; it does not seek to create a new economic system or heavily regulate capitalism. The Third Way is a much more pragmatic programme that takes globalization to be an unavoidable aspect of contemporary political and economic life. This broad programme was expressed by political commentators such as Giddens, Robert Reich, and Will Hutton, as well as articulated by Bill Clinton as President of the USA and Tony Blair as the Prime Minister of the UK. Many sub-sequent leftist parties have continued this reformist approach, even though the term "Third Way" is now less used.

Giddens' account of the Third Way programme focuses on the importance of using government policy to deviate from neo-liberal precepts and actively intervene to promote public investment and social stability. Giddens (1998: 111–28) points to the "social investment state" as being an alternative to the welfare state that advances a programme of "positive welfare" where efforts to develop a productive society through education, training and childcare are exercised by the state and an array of civil society initiatives. Essentially, governments ought to foster the skills needed for break-ing cycles of poverty in an increasingly capitalistic and technological context, rather than by supporting people with traditional welfare state entitlements. The welfare policies of the Third Way overlap considerably with an emphasis on the development of social stability and community. The building of community is not a new task for government, but the Third Way places extraordinary emphasis on both local and national forms of community. This "communitarian" agenda, as discussed within the US and Britain, is also evident in Giddens' (1998: 66) assertion of "no rights without responsibilities" and Clinton's (1996: 8) ideas of "opportunity, responsibility and community."

The international dimensions of the Third Way rhetorically sup-ported the idea of moderating global capitalism. As Giddens (1998: 129) contends, "the emerging global order cannot sustain itself as a 'pure marketplace'"; it requires the rule of law and effective global governance. This support of liberal internationalism, which was mirrored in some respects by the practices of the Blair and Clinton governments, is augmented in Giddens' (1998: 129, 152–3) work by references to the importance of forms of global governance able to act on economic stability and ecological risk. While the efforts of Blair and Clinton to address conflicts in Somalia and Balkans came under significant criticism for their selectivity and ulterior motives, they do point to the ways in which the Third Way does have an external dimension that incorporates a vision of "international community" (Blair 1999). By this Blair (1999) means that we are bearing witness to

> the explicit recognition that today more than ever before, we are mutu-ally dependent, that the national interest is to a significant extent gov-erned by international collaboration . . . Just as within domestic politics, the notion of community – the belief that partnership and co-operation

are essential to advance self-interest – is coming into its own; so it needs to find its international echo. Global financial markets, the global environment, global security and disarmament issues: none of these can be solved without intense international co-operation.

Nevertheless, despite rhetoric about a "far-reaching overhaul and reform of the system of international financial regulation" (Blair 1999), there seems to be significant limits to this conception of international community and the resolve of Third Way governments in particular (see Callinicos 2001: 109).

Consequently, the social democratic credentials of the Third Way have been actively contested (Giddens 2000). We can clearly see that the Third Way accepts the "core neo-liberal tenets" of the prevailing form of globalization (Callinicos 2001: 106), and does not generate the political will to regulate global finance or create a global consensus capable of moderating the social problems stemming from global capitalism. The Third Way ended up integrating some of the ideas of neo-liberalism within the Labour movement, which served the purpose of sustaining liberalism and capitalism. (Callinicos 2001: 8–12). Critics of the Third Way have thus dismissed it as being "Thatcherism pursued by other means" (Callinicos 2001: 3). Consequently, at a more fundamental level, while leftist and social democratic parties enacted the Third Way, the predominant philosophical underpinnings of the Third Way are liberal-capitalist not social democratic. As David Marquand (1999: 46) explains:

> the social liberal and social democratic traditions were not identical but they both held that the capitalist free market should be tamed in the interests of social citizenship and human flourishing. New Labour has turned that proposition inside out. Its aim is to re-engineer the society and culture so that the economy can compete more effectively in the global market place.

We can see, for example, that investments in education and health are desirable for the Third Way because they provide enhanced opportunities for the individual and for the economic prosperity for society, not because of any commitment to egalitarian notions of citizenship, human rights, or human welfare. Indeed, the idea that welfare mechanisms ought to serve these human purposes has slipped from common usage in many liberal societies since the rise of neo-liberalism. While the aim of Third Way policies on welfare, social cohesion as well as domestic and international political institutions is to adapt to the reality of economic globalization, not to significantly change its course, other strands of social democratic thought have advocated more significant challenges to global capitalism.

The first alternative position is that reformist social democracy does not have to mean the minimalist reforms advocated by the Third Way. Scholars such as Will Hutton and Colin Crouch have advocated changes to global capitalism that go beyond making workers competitive for transnational capital. In the 1990s, Hutton (1997: 90) critiqued the social exclusion of neo-liberalism in the UK and emphasized principles of inclusion and public involvement in his argument for a "stakeholder society" which actively considers the interests of all parties. Hutton (1997: 21) contended that this means the development of democratic forms of financial regulation, which "with proper democratic mechanisms would take a more rounded view of what constitutes efficiency and make a more pragmatic judgment about the balance between private and public interests." Such democracy would require the international re-invention of the arrangements of Bretton Woods to balance international capitalism with stability (Hutton 1996: 313). Colin Crouch (2013: 19) also demonstrates the possibility of reformist social democracy when he argues for the development of "assertive social democracy" which does not attempt to transcend capitalism but is more critical of neo-liberalism than the Third Way. This model rests upon regulating finance to prevent the formation of clusters of overwhelming corporate power to better achieve the prosperity and equality sought by social democrats. The development of this model requires engagement beyond the traditional working class and political parties via alliances with civil society networks of environmentalists, for instance (Crouch 2013: ch. 8). Both Hutton and Crouch indicate a connection with republican conceptions of citizenship which extends beyond the political sphere into the economic and social spheres.

A second alternative to the Third Way's conception of social democracy is evident in efforts to extend social democracy to the global level. While the state has been central to efforts to enact the social democratic vision, there have also been proposals to extend the international dimension of social democracy directly to global forms of governance. This is most evident in David Held's conception of cosmopolitan social democracy which advocates the democratization and regulation of global economic activity. Because economic processes operate globally, the realization of Held's cosmopolitan system (explained in Chapter 4) would have to be global and therefore embedded within cosmopolitan laws and policies influencing states and markets (Held 1995, 2004). Held is attentive to measures that address concentrations of corporate power and develop publicly determined private ownership limits for key public institutions such as the media. Furthermore, Held (1995: 280) also argues for the development of regulatory reforms which enable the redistribution of economic resources that are needed to enable a sense of economic autonomy through the provision of a minimum income as well as addressing "the most pressing cases of avoidable economic suffering and harm" (Held 1995: 256). These regulatory efforts also point toward a path that constrains markets from determining political outcomes and in turn provide a form of governance that offers better social opportunities and improved social protections than those proffered by neo-liberalism. In the contemporary context, this means challenging the core ideas of the Washington Consensus with a cosmopolitan social democratic program that seeks to publicly assist the excluded while ensuring that globalization works in more economically inclusive manner. This necessitates "international regulation with efforts to reduce the economic vulnerability of the poorest countries by transforming market access, eliminating unsustainable debt, reversing the outflow of net capital assets from the South to the North, and creating new facilities for development purposes" (Held 2004: 156). Such measures would eventually be underpinned by global citizens electing officials who would direct the constitution of global governance (see Chapter 4).

While Held circumvents the state for the development of social democracy, other social democrats also look at efforts to promote social purposes outside the state. A third alternative is evident in bottom-up programs of social democracy stemming from groups of people operating outside the state. In particular, Joe Guinan (2013) contends that social democrats need to move beyond their conventional focus upon the state and adopt a radical approach that embraces existing on-the-ground examples of democratic wealth ownership. This form of community-led democratic capital ownership includes "social enterprises that undertake businesses to support social missions; non-profit community development corporations (CDCs) and community land trusts that develop and maintain low-income housing; and community development financial institutions (CDFIs) that now invest more than $5.5 billion a year in creating jobs and housing and providing services for poor communities" (Guinan 2013: 16). As Guinan and others indicate, in the wake of the global financial crisis and the Eurozone crisis an "alternative economic sector" has developed where people attempt to disengage from markets and develop communal economic practices disconnected from global capitalism (Castells et al. 2012: 12). One key response to neo-liberalism and globalization, and an alternative to Third Way reformism, is to further develop these local forms of communal economic practice and enable social democratic states to encourage such practices.

Finally, the most dramatic alternative to the weak reformism of the Third Way's response to globalization is to embrace the socialist principles within the social democratic tradition and advance a radical program that aims to democratically plan economic activity. While various movements have advocated such a project, Alex Callinicos has most prominently articulated the contemporary promise and challenges of putting such a project into practice. Callinicos (2003: 95–8) suggests that since the rise of anti-capitalist movements in the mid-1990s, there appears to be significant momentum behind radical politics. However, this activity actually reveals a diverse and divided Left, as well as widespread skepticism that class has any meaningful agency within contemporary politics. Callinicos is keen to point to the importance of keeping a Marxist focus on class as the central driver in challenging and transcending global capitalism. Indeed, without transcending the logic of capitalism, reformist social democracy can only make temporary gains for the working class (Callinicos 2003: 121). A socialist transformation of the state is required to supersede the logic of capitalism and this requires a sustained revolution and mass struggles operating within an international movement animated by universalist principles of class struggle (Callinicos 2003: 112–14). The transformation of capitalism would entail the social ownership and democratic planning of all economic activity of each state in conjunction with global agreements animated by the revolutionary movement. This would require a "transitional program" involving various measures such as the regulation of global finance and the cancelation of debt, which have been articulated by existing anti-capitalist movements (Callinicos 2003: 140–2). Crucially, the revolutionary movement needs to keep democratic participation engaged within both global and national economic and political structures in order to ensure that the revolution does not backslide into weak reformism.

The Problems of Social Democracy

These contemporary social democratic responses to globalization demonstrate a wide range of possible political pathways to regulating the capitalist underpinnings of globalization and thus shifting policy-making away from neo-liberalism. While efforts to intervene

democratically in economic life to promote equality are not unique
to social democratic thought, such intervention being directed by the
state is the hallmark of social democracy. Nevertheless, there have
been longstanding criticisms of social democratic thought in both its
reformist and radical dimensions. A key issue is whether globalization
enhances or diminishes the influence of the social democratic agenda.
It could be argued that neo-liberalism has atomized society and fragmented the working class in many respects, which means classless
movements like the environmental and human rights movements are
the only contemporary agents for political change. However, it could
also be argued that neo-liberalism has failed to address social problems stemming from market failures and the centralization of wealth
– as evident graphically in the global financial crisis – which has led
to growing forms of public disquiet. Either way, it is now important
to consider the main issues concerning the viability and feasibility of
the social democratic response to neo-liberalism and globalization.

The central problem facing the social democratic tradition is its
global feasibility as an alternative to neo-liberalism and capitalism.
Specifically, how can social democratic ideas be articulated into
political practice at the national and global levels? The strengths of
the social democratic tradition are well known, just as the problems
and weaknesses of neo-liberalism are broadly discussed (Crouch
2013). Yet the realization of a strong account of reformist social
democracy or radical socialism does not appear to be an easy or
likely possibility. As Crouch (2013: 19) indicates, contemporary
social democracy does not have a "paucity of ideas, but a paucity
of power." The central issue is that there is no clear and consistent
agency actively supporting the social democratic proposal to regulate
global capitalism. The traditional political bases of social democracy
such as the working class, unions, leftist political parties and intellectuals appear to have a largely national focus on attempting to
influence the policy-making of the state. This is despite the attempts
of unions to develop global federations of unions and participate
more actively in transnational civil society – often referred to as social
movement unionism (Vandenberg 2007). While there are regions
and countries where the ideals of social democracy and socialism still
resonate strongly, the prospects of some global movement or revolution appears to be resisted by a number of factors.

First, a key issue facing the development of social democracy as a
response to globalization is the possibility and nature of democratic
leadership within both revolutionary and reformist responses to
globalization. While questions have long been expressed about the

democratic problems of directing and sustaining socialist revolutions, the contemporary problem of leadership rests more broadly upon whether social democratic leaders can change the nature of the state. Even with respect to the modest reformism of the Third Way, there were concerns about the technocratic and managerial nature of reforms. Other forms of social democratic thought also have a seemingly inherent commitment to the state and top-down leadership, which may produce policies that promote equality and democracy, but are nevertheless a form of elitism. Craig Browne (2006: 50) argues that this elitism reflects the "intention of realizing 'democratic' outcomes through forms of managerial direction" which "depends on a kind of technocratic justification, rather than arguments for extending democratic processes of participation." While this kind of statism has been "critical to the program of democratically regulating capitalism, statism seems limited in respect of the democratizing tendencies that have developed within civil society" (Browne 2006: 50). For both reformist and radical social democrats, then, the political project of promoting democratic restraints on capitalism must stop being what social democratic governments do and start being what people do (Lawson 2011). The challenge for social democratic thought is to conceive and sustain this form of democratic leadership emerging in civil society. From this angle, some anarchist scholars have argued that we need to delink radical politics from the state (see Chapter 7).

Problems with technocratic leadership take on different dimensions within the context of globalization. On the one hand, social democrats do need to wrest the state from neo-liberals and instil some faith in the state and its ability to develop public responses to public problems. But on the other hand, there is the danger expressed by Gamble (2010) that relying upon the state can lead to a simplistic view of politics that uses "state power to bring about the good society," which "sets up expectations which cannot be met and leads to swings between unrealistic hope and unfounded disillusion." In this view, the goal of social democrats should not be to develop a technocratic state that runs everything, but instead enable the kind of institutions and policies that can embed the social democratic values of fairness and equality into society (Gamble 2010; see also Lawson 2011). Clearly these institutions need to be developed beyond the state – but in a way that opens up public avenues of transparency and accountability. There is a danger in arguments for cosmopolitan social democracy that such efforts could continue to enhance technocracy by developing detached forms of governance in regional and global contexts (Browne 2006: 50–1). In short, while technocratic forms of leadership have been crucial to the realization of actual forms of social democracy, the question is whether these forms of top-down leadership are consistent with a project that seeks to develop public participation. In many respects, the project of enhancing transnational deliberation as argued by deliberative scholars like John Dryzek is an important counterpoint to social democratic thought in addition to liberal thought (see Chapter 5).

A second key point regarding the feasibility of the social democratic response to globalization relates to the intellectual resources that ought to guide efforts to develop social democracy. Across the history of social democratic thought, socialist and social democratic impulses have been closely connected to forms of political thought relating to republicanism, anarchism, and in more recent times, Green theory. Such relationships can be seen in form of parliamentary alliances and in social movements such as the anti-capitalism movement (Callinicos 2003: ch. 2). The question is what intellectual foundation is best for realizing social democracy in the contemporary era: a narrow and distinct account based strongly on socialist intellectual foundations and the working class; or upon alliances with various civil society critics of neo-liberalism. After all, while alliances may be strategically useful, social democrats need to consider whether they weaken social democratic ideals or make consistent efforts to regulate capitalism more likely. In this regard, we can see tensions in the anti-capitalism movement between groups desiring minor reforms and groups wanting more systematic transformation of capitalism (Callinicos 2003: ch. 2; Pleyers 2010). Consequently, some social democrats argue for the importance of local forms of political practice and collective ownership rather than relying upon indiscriminate global alliances with disparate interests (Martell 2011; Guinan 2013). Nevertheless, intellectual allies of social democracy have been making arguments critical of neo-liberalism consistent with those of strong reformists. For example, republican scholarship has sought to make the argument for regulating capitalism in line with the public good (Dagger 2006; S. Slaughter 2005) and Green theory has also been arguing for using the state to regulate economic activity (Eckersley 2004). As such, some social democratic scholarship argues there has been a "narrowing of social democracy" and that it needs to be broadened again, because "social democracy will be stronger in the future if it engages with other traditions such as republicanism – rediscovering new ways to define the public realm and the public interest – and cosmopolitanism, recovering the internationalism which one hundred years ago was its hallmark" (Gamble 2010; see also Crouch 2013: 1–3).

A third key point facing the future of social democracy is the nature and feasibility of a political community able to support a strong reformist or radical agenda. While social democracy has long had an internationalist component, the robust reform agenda that spurred the creation of welfare states across Europe was also based upon strongly nationalist forms of political community where high levels of taxation and regulation were deemed to produce public goods which benefitted the whole of society. While the Third Way articulated a support of nationalism, the position of contemporary social democratic scholarship has made connections with cosmopolitan, regional and transnational forms of political community. How can we reconcile the nationalist history of social democracy with its current cosmopolitan and transnational orientation? Clearly, most contemporary social democratic intellectuals consider inward nationalism to be a dead end for social democracy. As Luke Martell (2011) contends, social democracy needs to position itself "against populist nationalism not accommodate to it" and therefore:

> work with developing countries and social movements who have cosmopolitan values. And internationalism needs to work up from the power of example and practice rather than pursue abstract and unenforceable agreements from the top-down.

Furthermore, radical attempts to forge a revolution also need to consider these same dynamics by developing a clear transnational focus on the interests and activity of a working class shorn away from nationalism but shaped by something more than a radical identity of transnational protest and resistance disconnected from the state. There is also a tension between groups wanting to live out an alternative to neo-liberalism and those attempting to strategically reform or transform the institutions underpinning the global economy (Pleyers 2010). These challenges and disagreements about what purpose should underpin a radical or socialist conception of community are evident in various protest movements.

Conclusion

As this chapter has demonstrated, any effort to examine democratic theory and globalization would be incomplete without considering the social democratic and socialist arguments to regulate or transform global capitalism. The crucial challenge that social democracy presents to the theories considered thus far is to emphasize that globalization has powerful capitalist and neo-liberal underpinnings. These underpinnings powerfully shape the nature and limits of democracy, but often go unexamined in much of the contemporary democratic theory literature. This is not to say that social democrats have a singular approach to the democratic development of equality. Clearly, the divide between efforts to reform or overthrow global capitalism remains a crucial point of contention. Furthermore, despite emphasizing the importance of economics to democratic theory, there remain a range of challenging issues facing social democrats, including those socialist scholars who claim that democracy is only possible in world freed from the logic of capital. Questions relating to issues of leadership, alliances with related political traditions and the nature of social democratic political community are ongoing issues of debate. There are some radicals who contend that the social democratic tradition has been left vulnerable by the changing nature of domination in the contemporary world and that more radical options and social movements need to be constructed to abolish the state and political authority in a more broad-ranging sense. We turn to this radical anarchist scholarship in the next chapter.

Key Readings

Callinicos, A. (2003) *An Anti-Capitalist Manifesto*. Polity, Cambridge.
Crouch, C. (2013) *Making Capitalism Fit For Society*. Polity, Cambridge.
Gamble, A. (2009) Moving beyond the national: the challenges for social democracy in a global world. In Cramme, O. and Diamond, P. (eds.) *Social Justice in the Global Age*, Polity, Cambridge, pp. 117–35.
Giddens, A. (2000) *The Third Way and Its Critics*. Polity, Cambridge.
Held, D. (2004) *Global Covenant: The Social Democratic Alternative to the Washington Consensus*. Polity, Cambridge.

7
Radical Democracy

In September 2011, the Occupy movement revived a radical agenda aimed at challenging the injustices of finance capitalism and excessive corporate influence within representative democracies. The movement captured public attention with mass occupations of prominent sites of corporate power, including the Wall Street district in New York, and used these occupations as a platform to denounce rising inequality, fiscal austerity, corporate bailouts, and the disempowerment of "the 99 percent" in the wake of the 2008 global financial crisis. Rejecting traditional channels of political representation, the occupations experimented with direct forms of democracy in which consensual decision-making of equal citizens is the driving force shaping the conditions of their common life together. These experiments sought to create alternative democratic communities without any formal leadership or representative structures in order to prefigure a democratic future beyond the existing political order; an order that currently privileges business interests while excluding the overwhelming majority of citizens from direct participation in political decision-making. In so doing, the Occupy movement shed light on the vast inequities within contemporary liberal democracies and highlighted the enduring appeal of anarchist ideals of autonomy and "horizontal" politics within radical activist movements.

Against this background, this chapter examines the radical anarchist approach to global democracy, focusing on the work of Michael Hardt and Antonio Negri. Their approach is grounded in an ethic of revolution that seeks to develop autonomous, self-governing communities that can resist and overthrow the global system of sovereignty and its hierarchical capitalist relations. This radical approach argues that, when freed from the stifling perversions of sovereignty, the democratic potential of "the multitude" can be realized through the production of a commonwealth that is constituted by a political conception of love able to generate new forms of cooperation and affection, rather than a corrupted system of property relations. It thus offers a new theory of communism shaped by anarchist ideals and the promise of a post-sovereign world in which a self-organizing multitude is driven by love to share in the production of a common life together. The first section examines the radical perspective on globalization, focusing on the expansion of "imperial sovereignty" and the "fetters" placed on the full realization of human potential. The second section outlines the conceptual and normative framework of Hardt and Negri's "democracy of the multitude" and the revolutionary promise of "the common" as a space of liberation that can overcome the struggles over property that define modern politics. Finally, the chapter identifies a number of problems with this radical approach and its emphasis on an abstract articulation of "the multitude" with only the vaguest indications about the pathways toward, and organization of, a democratic future. Radical approaches confront a formidable array of political and economic actors with vested interests in sovereign politics and global capitalism that suggest a revolutionary shift to anarchist forms of democracy is a largely utopian goal under current conditions. In this context, it is argued that radicals cannot avoid important questions of political transition and dilemmas of representation and leadership if they wish to build a mass constituency for democratic change.

The Shackles of Imperial Sovereignty

For many radicals, the late twentieth century is recognized as the beginning of a novel "neo-liberal globalization" phase of capitalist production and market exchange that poses different problems and possibilities for democratic politics. Interestingly, this new situation has created fertile ground for anarchist conceptions of global democracy. When the Soviet Union's model of authoritarian communism collapsed and social democrats around the world later succumbed to the "Third Way" (see Chapter 6), "anarchism's major competitors for a theory of organization imploded" (Gitlin 2011). In this context, the decentralized and pluralistic nature of anarchism and its trenchant critique of authority seemed to provide radicals with an attractive model for connecting a wide range of anti-capitalist, anti-war, anti-nuclear, feminist, and environmental movements committed to resisting neo-liberal policies. The development of the Internet and electronic forms of social media also provided new possibilities for large-scale organization across continents without any centralized leadership or authority (Castells 2008). This made possible a loosely networked anti/alter-globalization "movement of movements" that became the main channel for expressing opposition to neo-liberal globalization, and entrenched anarchism as the "reigning spirit" within the radical left-wing groups that gave rise to the Occupy protests (Gitlin 2011).

The most important theoretical work in this revival of anarchism as a foundation for global democracy is contained in the trilogy of books written by Michael Hardt and Antonio Negri: *Empire* (2000), *Multitude* (2004), and *Commonwealth* (2009). Their starting point is the observation that contemporary globalization represents a fundamental historical shift to a global form of sovereignty called "Empire." Over the past several decades, the sovereignty of nation-states has declined with the "irresistible and irreversible" globalization of economic and cultural exchanges and the reduced capacity of states to regulate and impose their authority over them (Hardt and Negri 2000: xi). However, this does not mean that sovereignty itself has declined. Rather, sovereignty has taken a new *imperial* form in the political controls, state functions and regulatory mechanisms united under a single structure of rule that governs the entire world. This form of sovereignty is imperial in the sense that it involves a system of supranational authority that produces universal laws and standards of legitimacy that reach into the domestic realms of nation-states along all registers of social life. Specifically, imperial sovereignty is constituted at the global level by a new framework of "rights" producing norms and legal instruments of regulation and coercion that guarantee contracts, resolve conflicts, and justify intervention in the territories of subordinate national jurisdictions (Hardt and Negri 2000: 9–10). This is most clearly evident, for example, in the structural adjustment policies of the IMF and Western practices of humanitarian intervention that police compliance with global norms. Unlike the old imperialism of European colonial states, Empire has no territorial centre of power; its "networks of command" are without territorial limits and are directed by "global aristocracies" consisting of dominant capitalist nation-states, multinational corporations, global economic organizations, and regional supranational institutions (Hardt and Negri 2004: 320). The United States certainly commands a privileged placed in this imperial system, but no single nation-state can form the centre of an imperial sovereignty that is defined by the networked control of social order rather than territorial acquisition of foreign lands (Hardt and Negri 2000: xii).

This shift to imperial sovereignty has been accompanied by a transformation in the nature of capitalism. Specifically, there has been a significant change in its productive processes that has reduced the role of industrial factory labour and increased the priority of "biopolitical production" involving "communicative, cooperative, and affective labour" (Hardt and Negri 2000: 29). This production is *bio*political in the sense that it involves a form of power that encompasses and regulates the daily practices of social *life*. The biopolitical production of "immaterial goods" such as knowledge, information, codes, languages, images, services, and social relationships is now hegemonic in the global economy, and even in the places where the production of material commodities remains important, it is often brands, logos and symbolic uses that define their quality and add most value in the production process. For example, a diverse range of information, knowledge, and social relationships is produced using shared media platforms such as Fox News and Twitter, or through participation in global events such as Earth Hour and the World Social Forum. And the "surplus value" that is appropriated from material commodities ranging from computers to clothing is dictated by the corporate promotion of global brands and logos. This means that in the contemporary world the object of capitalist production is social life itself rather than just a realm of material things; education, health care, and prisons, for example, are premier sites of biopolitical production that have become vital places of capital accumulation (Harvey et al. 2009). From this perspective, Empire needs to be understood in terms of the "biopower" of a sovereign authority that controls the lives of populations through the production of social reality and, specifically, by defining how people think of themselves and others *as political subjects*. As David Harvey notes, if we are all neo-liberals now, that is because this is how our subjectivity has been produced by contemporary capitalism (Harvey et al. 2009).

In this context, financiers are the new masters of property that seek to appropriate biopolitical production and thus place "fetters" on the abilities and potential of people. According to Hardt and Negri (2012: 13), the financialization of global capitalism has transformed capital accumulation from an order based on the hegemony of profit generated through industrial exploitation, to one dominated by rent and accumulation of the value of common goods that are socially produced. For example, what makes Facebook an attractive investment is the social network that is generated by the common activities of people as they develop relationships and share information; activities from which rents can be extracted by financiers in the form of advertising revenue. Under finance capitalism, the "new poor" – which includes not only the unemployed and casual worker, but also precarious wage earners and the impoverished middle class – are primarily characterized by *chains of debt* (Hardt and Negri 2012: 10–14). The financier is primarily characterized as a rent-seeker who is external to the production process and blind to its injustices and oppressions. This distant rent-seeking and the financial control of life result in a new form of servitude that fails to engage and develop productive forces. Reminiscent of Marx's notion of alienation, Hardt and Negri (2009: 299) argue that contemporary capitalist relations of production fetter the abilities of ever greater portions of the global population. In Western countries, there has been "growth without jobs," and "in the subordinate regions an increasing number of people are becoming 'disposable,' useless from the perspective of capital." In a more general sense, they claim that few of those who are employed by capital "are allowed to develop their full productive capacities but are limited instead to routine tasks, far from their potential" (Hardt and Negri 2009: 299).

However, capitalist relations are not the only axis of domination that stifles human potential in the contemporary world. For Hardt and Negri (2004: xiii), the age of Empire is characterized not only by the hierarchies and injustices of global capitalism, but also by perpetual war: a global state of civil war that functions as an instrument of imperial rule. From this perspective, all of the world's armed conflicts – including those in Colombia, parts of Africa, Israel-Palestine, Iraq and Afghanistan – should be considered imperial wars that exist within, and are conditioned by, the biopower of Empire in order to control populations and reproduce a hierarchical social order (Hardt and Negri 2004: 4, 13). This is also true of the struggles against domination based on race, gender and sexuality that are waged in the guise of politics but are simply "war conducted by other means" (Hardt and Negri 2009; Foucault 2004: 48). Capitalist domination certainly plays a role in creating and sustaining these other forms of domination but does not adequately account for their specific nature. For Hardt and Negri (2004: 17), justice and democracy do not belong in this global state of affairs: war requires strict hierarchy and obedience and thus the partial or total suspension of democratic participation. That is, when war is a permanent condition, the suspension of democracy becomes the norm rather than the exception. Following John Dewey, they argue that the current global state of war "forces all nations, even those professedly most democratic, to become authoritarian and totalitarian" (Hardt and Negri 2004: 18). Torture and surveillance, for example, are considered unavoidable and justifiable techniques of power for both dictatorships and liberal democracies (Hardt and Negri 2004: 19).

A central facet of this anti-democratic nature of Empire is the failure of modern models of "bourgeois representation." According to Hardt and Negri (2011), liberal democratic politics is subservient to economic and financial interests and the politicians and political parties charged with representing the people's interests in fact more clearly represent banks and creditors. Socialist alternatives have fared no better. The claim of the "vanguard party" to represent the working class in many socialist societies of the twentieth century was increasingly degraded as citizen participation was excluded from institutions of state authority, and as central governments led by the Soviets became increasingly authoritarian. In this context, East European regimes were unable to sustain the fiction that their institutions were any more representative than their liberal competitors. Hardt and Negri (2004: 252) argue that the eventual implosion of these regimes was due to a conceptual problem: socialism and communism did not develop different conceptions of representation, "and as a result they repeated the founding nucleus of the bourgeois conception of sovereignty, trapped paradoxically in the need for the unity of the state." Like liberal democracies, socialists could not dispense with the need for a centralized state apparatus to manage capital and thus reproduced similar hierarchical organs of representation to mediate, control, and express social interests. As such, this modern form of bourgeois representation is unable to correct "the general crisis of democratic representation in global society" in which dominant nation-states exert control over the UN and economic organizations such as the IMF, and the representative character of NGOs and global civil society is very weak (Hardt and Negri 2004: 264, 290–6). The construction of a global parliament in this context is not only unfeasible due to the intransigence and unilateralism of great powers like the US, but also requires new thinking about representative politics because the leap to the global scale undermines all old models of representation (Hardt and Negri 2004: 295). That is, global democracy based on biopolitical production requires us to invent "new forms of democracy that go beyond representation" (Hardt and Negri 2004: 255). In this sense, the radical perspective echoes the views of earlier participatory democrats that wish to build "stronger" democracies in which the direct participation of citizens is at the very centre of democratic life (Barber 1984; Pateman 1970).

For Hardt and Negri, then, processes of globalization have resulted in the extension of imperial sovereignty and new fetters on the full development of human potential, but also generate the foundation of biopolitical production where revolutionary struggles and an alternative political organization can be constructed. This alter-globalization, or counter-Empire, must destroy the power of money and the financial bonds it creates and replace them with new social bonds that allow the full development of people through the social production of common goods. These social bonds must be constructed outside of the "republic of property" and reappropriate the common goods that finance now possesses. From this perspective, reformist accounts of the social democratic project (see Chapter 6) are manifestly inadequate because they consist of the illusory aim to "reintegrate the working class within capital" without recognizing that reforming the republic of property will never lead to equality and freedom (Hardt and Negri 2009: 17–20). Indeed, all contemporary politics, as it is conventionally defined, is a struggle with control over property as its central axis: "the concept of property and the defence of property remain the foundation of every modern political constitution" (Hardt and Negri 2009: 15). The logic of revolution in this context is that the contradiction between the private nature of capitalist property relations and the social nature of biopolitical production is unsustainable. Thus, an alternative form of globalization must overthrow the republic of property underpinning Empire in order to construct a real democracy of the multitude.

The Democracy of the Multitude

For Hardt and Negri (2004: 340), contemporary global politics involves war, domination, alienation, and expropriation, but its characteristic mode of biopolitical production also provides the seeds of resistance and common arenas through which democracy can be truly realized for the first time. A new project of democracy is thus only imaginable on the global scale and is necessary because "no other path will provide a way out of the fear, insecurity, and domination that permeates our world at war; no other path will lead us to a peaceful life in common" (Hardt and Negri 2004: xii). The basis for this new democracy lies in existing grievances concerning the corruption of finance capitalism and political representation, and diverse struggles concerning class, gender, sexuality, and race, and other axes of oppression that must be organized in project of liberation. As such, "the multitude" is required to creatively invent and autonomously construct modes of "constituent power" to subvert and transcend Empire. This anarchist approach thus hinges on a detailed account of the conceptual and normative underpinnings of "the multitude" and its revolutionary activities in "the common."

The central idea that underpins the anarchism of Hardt and Negri is that true democracy requires the multitude to rule itself autonomously without domination by hierarchical authorities. Here, the multitude does not mean "the people," or "the masses," or indeed any concept that reduces the innumerable internal differences of human beings to a unified identity or an incoherent aggregate. Rather, the multitude is composed of networks of "singularities": "social subjects whose differences cannot be reduced to sameness" and are therefore unrepresentable as a unified whole (Hardt and Negri 2004: 99). That is, singularities refer to people that are defined by their numerous relationships to others in society and consist of internal differences that change over time (see Hardt and Negri 2009: 338–9). People develop as human beings in a variety of social settings that produce a multiplicity of experiences, social roles, and internal partitions that cannot be reduce to a single overarching identity. This is evident when people act on different (and sometimes contradictory) interests, opinions and beliefs in different social situations; interests, opinions and beliefs that change over the course of their lives. For example, many people around the world want nationalist policies to protect their language from the global spread of English, yet also reveal cosmopolitan beliefs in their support for charities that help the global poor. Many citizens vote for parties that promise action on climate change, yet drive a car to work each day. This makes it impossible to represent human beings as entire selves or centres of consciousness (Cole 1920: 105–6). Conversely, Hardt and Negri (2009: 7) do not conceive of singularities in terms of "the individual," which they argue is a liberal construction that underpins and justifies competition within a capitalist republic of property.

The multitude is thus a network of self-organizing singularities that converge in the production of common goods like languages, knowledge, and social relationships. The multitude is poor, but this poverty is not associated with deprivation or misery. Rather, the poverty of the multitude is defined by *an absence of property* that makes possible a radically plural and inclusive body politic that is open to all those involved in social production (Hardt and Negri 2009: 39–45). The most fully developed example of the organization of the multitude is found in the global cycle of struggles that emerged around issues of globalization in the late 1990s. A distributed global network arose from the WTO protests in Seattle and Genoa, riots in South East Asia against IMF policies, the Zapatista rebellion in Mexico, and Indian farmers' protests, to name a few, and reemerged and widened during the more recent Arab uprisings, Spanish encampments and Occupy movement. In this network, each local struggle functions as a node that communicates with other nodes without any hub or centre of intelligence, thereby remaining singular and tied to local conditions but also immersed in a common web (Hardt and Negri 2004: 217). The democratic promise of the multitude thus lies in the plurality, dynamism and autonomy of its singularities and their capacity to participate in "the common." In an age of biopolitical production, its central tools are "no longer the spinning loom or cotton gin or metal press, but rather linguistic tools, affective tools for constructing relationships, tools for thinking, and so forth" (Hardt and Negri 2009: 308).

The fundamental normative emphasis of this approach thus lies in the production of "the common" as a revolutionary space of democratic relations. As indicated above, the common springs from contemporary social life in which the hegemony of immaterial labour is transforming the organization of production from the linear and hierarchical relationships of the assembly line to the worldwide webs of the information age. As such, it means something more than natural resources such as the atmosphere, the oceans, and other common resources on earth; it also encompasses what is socially produced and shared: ideas, images, languages, relationships, experiences, and a variety of other social practices. Although currently degraded and consumed by capitalism, the common is grounded in forms of communication and cooperation that produce horizontal relationships that tend to escape the clutches of hierarchical authority and thus can be mobilized to resist the biopower of Empire. Indeed, drawing on Baruch Spinoza, Hardt and Negri (2004: 311) argue that democratic relations form the basis of the vast majority of our political, economic, affective, linguistic and productive interactions; democratic interactions are in fact the basis of our living in common that makes society possible. This is evident in the common wealth of the contemporary metropolis – "the factory for the production of the common" – which consists not only of a built environment of buildings, streets and parks, but also a living dynamic of cultural practices, intellectual circuits, affective networks, and social institutions (Hardt and Negri 2009: 154, 250). Indeed, for Hardt and Negri (2009:

250), "the metropolis is to the multitude what the factory was to the industrial working class." This means global cities such as New York, London, Shanghai, Tokyo, and Mumbai are the primary sites of revolutionary struggle.

This understanding of the common should not be equated with a "public" realm that is fenced by the constitution of a state and policed by the constituted power of its institutions. The common resists constitutionalization because democratic communities involved in biopolitical production cannot be bounded by territorial borders or politically frozen in time. Indeed, constitutionalism is a theory of limited government involving the mediation of inequality and therefore a practice that limits democracy (Negri 1999: 2). The common, however, is always being remade by the "constituent power" of the multitude. For Negri (1999: 11), constituent power is the door through which the multitude's democratic will enters politics as it seeks to burst apart, break, interrupt and unhinge any pre-existing equilibrium. The desire for community is "the spirit of constituent power," and love is the driving force that allows people to escape the solitude of individualism and participate in the production of the common (Negri 1999: 11; Hardt and Negri 2009: 179–88). This political conception of love involves a process by which we expand our relationships and extend our care to others to produce new forms of social solidarity, affective networks, and schemes of cooperation. A love of humanity, for example, underpins many collective projects and social movements to improve the lives of strangers living in extreme poverty. Love is what pulls the common together and allows the multitude to produce new and revolutionary understandings of their social relations. However, Hardt and Negri's conception of love is not to be confused with its "corrupted" forms that limit love to those who have the same identity. What passes for love today in ordinary discourse and popular culture, they argue, is predominantly this corrupted form. Family, race, and nation, for example, are corruptions of the common that require us to love those most like us to the exclusion or subordination of those outside (Hardt and Negri 2009: 182). Overcoming these corruptions and adopting a political sense of love does not mean we cannot love our partners, children or fellow nationals; it simply means that love does not end there, that love serves as the basis for political projects in the common and the construction of a new society (Hardt and Negri 2004: 352). Setting boundaries around love suppresses the potential of singularities and their production of an expanding democratic common.

This theoretical framework focuses on the democratic potential of the multitude while resisting prescriptions that would "codify new social relations in a fixed order" (Hardt and Negri 2012: 7). As such, Hardt and Negri limit their reflections on global democratization to three broad pathways that can organize the constituent power of the multitude. First, as a precondition for the multitude to rule itself, sovereignty must be "destroyed." As Hardt and Negri (2004: 353) put it, "sovereignty in all its forms inevitably poses power as the rule of one and undermines the possibility of full and absolute democracy." While in the past communists and anarchists focused on the abolition of the state, today sovereignty must be abolished at the state and global levels in order to remove artificial fetters on democratic expression. Indeed, the autonomy of the multitude and its capacities for economic, political, and social self-organization eliminate any positive role for sovereignty in today's world (Hardt and Negri 2004: 340). Under these conditions, the destruction of sovereignty must be accompanied by new democratic structures composed of new checks and balances, rights and guarantees. While avoiding institutional design, Hardt and Negri (2009: 306–11) outline some possible reforms that would pave the way, including: new physical infrastructure for the entire global population to access safe and affordable food and water, basic sanitary conditions, electricity and a clean environment to support life; "a global education initiative" which provides mandatory education for all; an open infrastructure of information and culture; sufficient funds to meet technological requirements of advanced research; freedom of movement; a minimum guaranteed income for all regardless of work; and the establishment of mechanisms of participatory democracy at all levels of government.

Second, this radical approach sees existing movements based on class, gender, sexuality and race identities as the sites of revolutionary democratization. In contrast to many orthodox Marxists who focus upon the working class (see Chapter 6), all of these parallel "fields of struggle" have a role to play in the revolution against imperial sovereignty. As indicated above, Hardt and Negri do not consider capital to be the exclusive axis of domination, and therefore overthrowing capitalist rule is not the only mode of revolutionary activity (Harvey et al. 2009). The task for the multitude in this context is to organize the "intersections and encounters" of these struggles in a common project of liberation that retains the autonomy of each and avoids the temptation to represent them in a single unifying identity. Unification is a recipe for ceding control to an elite leadership that inevitably privileges one social group over others in the revolutionary struggle. Indeed, the ultimate goal of revolutionary change for these social movements is to transcend their identities and remake themselves as social subjects. Identity politics is the primary vehicle for struggle within and against the republic of property since identity itself is based on property and sovereignty (Hardt and Negri 2009: 326). Struggles based on national, race, and gender identities often involve overlapping demands for autonomous control over territory (e.g. separatist movements), or the redistribution of resources (e.g. reparations for indigenous dispossession), or access to representative offices (e.g. gender quotas). In this process, identity itself becomes the property of the struggle to be defended by hierarchically controlling members and excluding outsiders, often violently. As such, identity politics must be carried forward toward a revolutionary project: to strive for its own abolition (Hardt and Negri 2009: 332). Democracy of the multitude must involve a positive movement of self-transformation and metamorphosis toward new social subjects, eliminating the hierarchical structures and institutions upon which identities of class, race, gender and sexuality are built.

Finally, fostering the democratic organization of the multitude requires autonomy from both private/capitalist and public/state authority; it requires what Hardt and Negri (2009: 303) call an "exodus from the republic of property." They argue that it is no longer necessary for the capitalist or the state to organize production from the outside. This intervention merely disrupts and corrupts the processes of self-organization already functioning within the multitude (Hardt and Negri 2009: 302). As such, this pathway to democracy dovetails with traditional anarchist politics that distrusts traditional hierarchies, contains a disinterest in taking or influencing state power, and prefers "transgression" rather than counter-hegemonic efforts (Foust 2010: 2). It is evident in the prefigurative politics of the Occupy movement that seeks to create living examples of direct democracy and consensus processes that refuse to engage with established authorities and reject the role of the state in any revolutionary transition. In this sense, Hardt and Negri's democracy of the multitude, like most contemporary forms of anarchism, "is not so much a theory of the absence of government, but a theory of self-organization, or direct democracy, *as* government" (Gitlin 2011). Only when the multitude is freed from imperial sovereignty can it develop democratic decision-making that is able to govern the cooperation and conflict that emerges in the production of the common. This means global democracy will spring from the revolutionary spaces that are created when parallel struggles occur in local and transnational contexts against the social hierarchies of class, gender, race and sexuality and intersect to form new democratic powers and institutions independent from the modern politics of property.

Revolution without a Manifesto

Hardt and Negri offer a utopian vision of global democracy based on a theoretical elaboration of "the multitude" and "the common," and the identification of broad pathways for their emergence in a democratic future. This conceptual and normative framework is not a manifesto that calls into being a new subject as the agent of change so that it can enact a concrete institutional blueprint (Hardt and Negri 2012: 1). It is the constituent power of the multitude that makes democracy, so precise institutional forms cannot be detailed in advance. As such, this highly abstract approach poses a number of problems for those looking for concrete proposals and specific organizational plans that can be used to democratize global politics. While Hardt and Negri's theoretical discussions have made an important contribution to radical scholarship, their emphasis on conceptualizing the multitude and the common in abstraction from detailed accounts of practical politics means that their theories are of more limited use to citizens and social movements attempting to create the new constituent process they call for. Radicals on the ground do not have a philosophical blank slate on which to build democracy; they operate in political contexts that require goals and strategies about how to create a mass constituency for democratic change that can reform or overthrow the undemocratic powers that be.

From this angle, the radical anarchist approach seems directed at changing society through the propagation of new ideas and their voluntary adoption by society at large. This radical idealism seems to hinge on identifying the theoretical lenses for understanding latent democratic possibilities, rather than the more "scientific" strategy advocated by Marx aimed at developing detailed analyses of empirical conditions as basis for criticism and "realistic" strategies of revolution. As such, Marx and Engels (1967 [1848]: 115–17) dismissed the idealist approach and its refusal to engage with and adapt to existing power structures as "utopian socialism." To be sure, Hardt and Negri locate their arguments in a context of globalization in which imperial sovereignty and biopolitical production have become hegemonic. This means Marx's strategy of centralized, hierarchical revolution aimed at gaining state power must give way to a more "realistic" strategy of decentralized, horizontal revolution aimed at constructing new forms of society outside of state authority. The problem here is that Hardt and Negri's emphasis on abstract philosophical elaboration can only gesture toward the democratic *potential* of emerging forms of labour and struggle that are corrupted by present conditions. Without a developed account of a feasible political transition, however, the leap from the reality of Empire to the utopia of the multitude rests on a *promise* that historically unique conditions of production can herald a new kind of society with the power to remake the world order. This does not provide much practical guidance about how to convert presently corrupted biopolitical labour into common forms of life that can subsequently expand into a global movement for the elimination of sovereignty and capitalism. This radical anarchist approach seems to rely on convincing people that they have a historically unique opportunity to transcend their corrupted lives and demand post-sovereign democratic alternatives. But many people will want more than abstract promises if they are to seek an alternative form of life rather than simply demand a greater share within the existing order.

Where Hardt and Negri (2009: 164) do provide some guidance, it involves an "exodus" from modern politics: "the multitude must flee the family, the corporation and the nation" associated with the republic of property. They recognize that many people will be reluctant to accept a notion of class struggle as exodus (Hardt and Negri 2009: 164). Indeed, Bruce Robbins (2010) argues that "it makes more sense to think of the task of politics as staying to fight, and it makes more sense to think of the common as what is fought for." That is, the common is achieved when people succeed in creating and defending activities (such as wilderness preservation, access to genetic material, open source software, and Internet freedoms) against appropriation by sovereigns and capitalists. Hardt and Negri (2009: 164) acknowledge that exodus involves reappropriating the common as the "field of battle." But it is difficult to imagine how this can be successful without engaging with and actively confronting established power structures and political institutions. A strategy of exodus might involve withdrawing support for existing parliaments by not voting, boycotting corporations, and refusing debt offered by banks, but the "new world" of the common must also be actively protected and eventually break the "shell of the old" (Marx and Engels 1967 [1848]: 13). Hardt and Negri assume that if the multitude autonomously develops capabilities to manage its production, then politics will look after itself (Callinicos 2010).

The flight from modern politics can perhaps be explained by Hardt and Negri's wish to escape to an alter-modern and natural common unspoiled by any contact with Empire. In direct contrast to Hobbes' war among the multitude, they assume human interactions outside of sovereignty will be self-organizing, leaderless, peaceful, and consist of a political form of love that is unlimited. That is, Hardt and Negri (2009: 191) are not concerned with feasible changes based on current social relations, but with "what human nature can become." The dynamics of developing transnational and transcultural forms of solidarity are also evident in attempts to fashion "postmodern global democracies" (Scholte 2014: 6) and in the actual practices of social movements contesting neo-liberalism (Pleyers 2010). The assumption is that freedom in the common can be created and safeguarded without any forms of political authority or formal constitutional arrangements; an assumption that is deeply contested by liberal internationalists and cosmopolitan democrats (see Chapters 3 and 4). Many liberals argue that a state or supranational authority is required to uphold the rule of law and protect the rights of citizens against abuses of power, especially those committed by majorities. Hardt and Negri simply associate these forms of political authority with sovereignty and the Hobbesian "rule of one" without engaging with the literature in previous chapters that views sovereignty as an increasingly limited, complex and disaggregated set of practices. This begs a crucial question: without a system of political authority, how will a multitude of singularities deal with transgressors who break the rules, or abuse their power, or engage in violent conflict? Once again, assuming life without sovereignty will simply eliminate this question constitutes a huge leap of faith.

The issue of organization is also central to the Hardt and Negri reforms to socio-economic infrastructure, education and political participation that would take us toward a more democratic future. Anarchists argue that "traditional organizational forms based on unity, central leadership, and hierarchy are neither desirable nor effective" (Hardt and Negri 2009: 166). If these goals are to be realized outside of existing political structures, however, there is no indication how horizontal self-organizing communities would undertake the massive project of global economic distribution without some kind of vertical administrative and leadership structure. Indeed, as David Harvey argues, the presumption that the world's population "can be fed, warmed, clothed, housed and cleaned without any hierarchical form of governance and outside the reach of monetization and markets is dubious in the extreme" (Harvey et al. 2009: 212). For anarchists, including Hardt and Negri (2012: 84–100), the solution to problems of global scale lies in the organizational principle of *federalism*. This does not mean a central authority ruling over smaller political units, but rather the free association of self-managed, directly democratic communities with delegate representation for levels of coordination higher than the local level (Chomsky 2002: 222). The state is replaced with a "commune of communes" with progressively higher levels of delegate representation that stretch from the local neighbourhood to the national and global levels.

These practical problems concerning political organization can be fleshed out by examining the Occupy movement, the closest expression of radical anarchist ideas in recent years. The philosophy of Occupy is based on "horizontalism" in which there is no formal leadership or hierarchical structure, only collective solidarities and loose interconnections maintained through Internet communication and de-centralized decisions made with the collective consent of local groups. In the Occupy camps, decision-making took place in general assemblies and workshops where activists collectively debated proposals for direct action and self-organization. Decisions were made by consensus, which in practice was produced by encouraging vehement dissenters to stand aside or to introduce super-majority voting for some issues (usually 90 percent agreement) (#Occupy London 2013; Muldoon 2012: 9–10). Furthermore, Occupy cannot be identified with a single overarching set of demands. Indeed, the very concept of issuing demands is rejected because it "means recognizing the legitimacy – or at least the power – of those of whom the demands are made" (Byrne 2012: 144).

The Occupy movement has demonstrated the difficulties in making these kinds of communities work. First, the strategy of shunning existing politics failed to generate a mass constituency for democratic change. The shift from protesting against the existing system to prefiguring democratic alternatives that occurred in New York seems to have limited the appeal of Occupy Wall Street among most Americans who prefer to express concrete grievances and demands within the existing representative system (Roberts 2012: 757). This was perhaps due to the fact that many of the general assemblies were prone to long, unwieldy debates focusing on camp management and other trivial topics rather than on making decisions about demands or direct action (Byrne 2012: 178; Muldoon 2012: 39). Second, Occupy demonstrated that democratic self-management of "a new world within an old shell" does not eliminate the vagaries and prejudices of social relations and itself requires highly organized forms of governance. For example, women occupiers in Melbourne were often denied full participation in assemblies and some experienced sexual harassment without any opportunity to rectify the problem (Muldoon 2012: 18). Some camps also struggled to manage more frequent reports of criminal violence, vandalism, theft, and drug dealing. Confronted with these problems, a determination to maintain and defend camps around the clock undermined support as occupiers faced burnout and fatigue, safety issues, divisions between campers and non-campers, and importantly, the gradual eclipse of their core mission to protest the harms done by neo-liberal politics. As such, the municipal authorities may have done the occupiers an unintended favour by shutting down the protest sites (Byrne 2012: 400). As Alasdair Roberts (2012: 757) argues, the "experiment with horizontalism was terminated before it could be seen to fail."

Finally, Occupy highlighted that even directly self-governing democracies must grapple with issues of representation and leadership. In principle, many Occupy protestors explicitly shun any form of representative politics or formal leadership. "No one represents us" was a popular cry in #Occupy Slovenia and there is a widespread denouncement of political representation as the corrupt outsourcing of political engagement (Razsa and Kurnik 2012: 239). At the same time, however, the movement also claims to represent the 99 percent and to empower "individuals to lead others into action by gathering in the commons" (#OccupyTogether 2013). These claims were increasingly challenged as growing numbers of people turned away from the assemblies, highlighting concerns about the extent to which participants represented the diversity of the 99 percent. In New York and Boston, despite the presence of a diverse range of people at daytime protests, significant numbers of overnight campers were white, young, and well-educated (Juris 2012: 265). This problem was exacerbated because a fear of cooptation meant occupiers tended to shun working with existing representative organizations, including unions, elected politicians and other traditional social movements with similar goals, which could have been used to help mobilize public support, establish greater representative connections to the 99 percent, and build mutually beneficial pressure for change. Moreover, Occupy appears to need a greater capacity to coordinate action through the development of leadership functions. This does not necessarily entail the creation of a centralized representative organization with a hierarchical leadership structure. In representative democracies, civil society leaders have an important communicative role in framing and politicizing social problems and diagnosing solutions in order to mobilize a mass constituency for change (Bray

2011: 179–82). Indeed, some deliberative theorists point to ways that civil society leaders can act as representers of specific voices and causes without the creation of hierarchical or electoral institutions (see Chapter 5). Leadership in this context is about coordinating a strategy that is able to articulate a succinct and coherent vision of economy and society as a broadly appealing alternative to the existing system.

The strength of the Occupy movement lies in its ability to disrupt routine politics by calling attention to issues of inequality and excessive corporate influence over representative democracy (Bray 2014). After the evictions, Occupy activism relies on social media networks to mobilize smaller protests and shorter occupations on issues such as banking reform, housing foreclosures, student debt, electoral reform, corporate accountability, campaign finance, and an array of local issues in cities around the world. Despite some successes in disrupting the activities of financial institutions and preventing foreclosures in the US, these victories are largely symbolic given the scale of finance capitalism and the continuing dominance of the neo-liberal agenda. Nevertheless, Occupy and other social movements contesting neo-liberal policies and global inequality have recently demonstrated that appeals to "the global poor" or "the 99 percent" can create important shifts in public discourse that could inspire democratic transformations in the future. For Hardt and Negri, it is these shifts in the way we understand society and our relations with one another that lie at the very heart of possible pathways to revolution.

Conclusion

The radical approach outlined by Hardt and Negri and evident in the practical politics of the Occupy movement is fundamentally concerned with building direct democracies on a global scale outside of the corrupting influence of sovereignty and capitalism. As Hardt and Negri acknowledge, their approach focuses on a multitude in the making that is only faintly identifiable in various struggles around the world. It thus remains an intentionally incomplete picture of how democracy without sovereignty should be organized in practice. This means that difficult practical questions remain about the strategy of a transitional politics; how to create collective action on a global scale among discrete self-governing communities; how material and immaterial public goods at all levels would be produced and distributed; and how new individual and collective rights would be realized and enforced in a highly decentralized world order. If we accept, as anarchists do, that the answers to these questions must emerge organically through the democratic processes of the multitude, then the overtly prescriptive function of global democratic theory evident in previous chapters is abandoned and its practical usefulness is limited. From this angle, Hardt and Negri's simple yet colossal project is to help create a revolutionary process that allows the multitude to recognize and remake their social relations while fostering future innovations and remaining open to new democratic directions.

Key Readings

Hardt, M. and Negri, A. (2000) *Empire*. Harvard University Press, Cambridge, MA, and New York.

Hardt, M. and Negri, A. (2004) *Multitude: War and Democracy in the Age of Empire*. The Penguin Press, New York.

Hardt, M. and Negri, A. (2012) *Declaration*. Argo-Nevis, New York.

Harvey, D., Hardt, M., and Negri, A. (2009) Commonwealth: an exchange. *Artforum International* 48 (3): 210–21.

Pleyers, G. (2010) *Alter-Globalization: Becoming Actors in the Global Age*. Polity, Cambridge.

Conclusion:
Global Democratic Theory
and the Citizen

The impact of globalization on democracy and the nation-state has provoked a wide array of responses from democratic theorists. As we have seen in previous chapters, the approaches of liberal internationalism, cosmopolitan democracy, transnational deliberative democracy, social democracy, and radical democracy develop considerably different democratic ethics and therefore different accounts of how democracy ought to respond to globalization. While these approaches are drawn from distinct and pre-existing political theories, they are also part of common body of scholarship responding to globalization that is referred to in this book as global democratic theory. Despite the differences between these approaches, there are some recurring themes in the literature about the deficiencies of the prevailing form of liberal democracy located within the state, and the possibilities of promoting democracy at the global level by transforming global governance and enhancing the participation of transnational civil society. It is thus important to consider these approaches in relation to each other and establish more dialogue between the positions in order to advance these debates. Drawing on this scholarship, this conclusion considers the ways in which the approaches analyzed in this book can assist in the future realization of democracy in the contemporary age of globalization and global governance. Its main contention is that global democratic theory needs to deliver a range of practical perspectives that can help democratic leaders and citizens to critically rethink and redesign the organization of national and global governance. In order to demonstrate its value in this regard, the conclusion outlines the animating concerns of global democratic theory, its major areas of agreement and disagreement, and identifies the most important design choices on the paths toward a more democratic future on a global scale.

Global Democratic Theory

The importance of global democratic theory as a body of scholarship originates from widespread agreement among scholars of democratic theory, political theory and International Relations that globalization is challenging democracy within the nation-state and opening up new opportunities for participation in global governance. As such, global democratic theory shares with much of democratic and political theory an underlying appreciation of the value of public rule and an intent to create and enhance avenues for collective public action that avoid the dangers of oligarchy or dictatorship. The guiding concerns for global democratic theory are therefore to identify the problems that globalization poses for democracy and to articulate how existing processes and institutions can be changed in order to enable democratic politics with global horizons. Generally speaking, all scholars see the existing mechanisms of global governance as inadequate from their particular democratic perspective. But interestingly, for most scholars a common concern with avoiding the centralization of power and its oppressive tendencies also leads to a rejection of world government. This means that global democratic theory sits in a normative space between existing global governance and a prospective world government consisting of a range of perspectives that vary widely in their desired level of change. Liberal internationalism, for example, offers quite modest suggestions about reforming global governance to make it accountable to national democracies, whereas cosmopolitan democracy suggests quite significant changes to the scope of political community and the institutional architecture required for democracy to operate at a global level. The radical perspective of Michael Hardt and Antonio Negri argues for more fundamental changes to the global order such as the eradication of sovereignty and capitalism in order to create a global anarchist democracy.

Global democratic theory is constituted by these different responses to the impact of globalization on democracy. The preceding chapters have examined the central problems that each approach seeks to address, outlined their key normative claims, and considered some of the prominent questions regarding their desirability and feasibility. As outlined in Table 1, what animates each approach is a distinct normative vision that defines the aspirations of democracy and leads to a particular vision of what democracy can and ought to look like. This involves some coherence around the core problem that globalization poses for democracy as well as normative claims regarding the location of democratic authority, the

Table 1: Global Democratic Theory

	Liberal Internationalism	Cosmopolitan Democracy	Transnational Deliberative Democracy	Social Democracy	Radical Democracy
Central problem posed by globalization	"Governance trilemma": we need global rules without centralized power but with government actors who can be held to account	Reconfiguration of power and authority has eroded the democratic autonomy of individuals	Lack of public participation and deliberation in global governance	Exploitation, inequality and domination associated with global capitalism	The fetters on human potential imposed by the global regime of imperial sovereignty
Location of democratic authority (who/what wields power on the basis of democratic credentials)	National officials representing a liberal democratic state	Global cosmopolitan law	Global and transnational public spheres	Nation-state guided by the activity and agents of the working class	Constituent power of the multitude without hierarchical authority

Scope and nature of political community (the boundaries of democratic politics)	Constitutionally limited national demos	All-affected on a global scale	Transnational communities of deliberation and communication	National, with some regard for international movement of the working class	Multitude of singularities participating in the common
Institutional form (what provides the structure of global rules?)	Nation-states participating in international organizations and government networks	Global constitution incorporating multi-level representative legislatures	Networks of transnational communication	State	Social networks of production from the local to the global
Central criticism of the theory	Creates a global technocracy of governmental networks largely beyond the reach of national democratic publics	Little consideration of political pathways for generating democracy beyond the state	Limited capacity of transnational deliberation to influence international institutions and political authority	Questionable global feasibility of the social democratic alternative to neo-liberal capitalism	Abstraction from the practical politics of transition and dilemmas of leadership and representation

scope and nature of political community, and institutional form of democracy. There is also coherence in the literature about the main problems with each approach. However, it is clear that key authors within each approach have their own detailed accounts that differ in some respects from others that share their broad vision. Recognizing these differences, this typology aims to identify and organize broad responses to globalization, not to simplify or ignore key political positions within or beyond these accounts. Indeed, while each approach possesses a high degree of coherence around a distinct normative vision, the differences *within* these approaches are often just as important as the differences between them, especially with regard to programs for implementing their particular visions in practice. For instance, transnational deliberative democrats agree that the deliberative capacities of those agents involved in global politics must be enhanced, but disagree about whether meaningful deliberation must utilize formal institutions or rely on the more freeform interactions of transnational civil society. Also, social democrats agree upon a vision of equality, but disagree on whether this must be realized by reforming capitalism or through a revolution which supplants capitalism.

Despite the diversity of responses in global democratic theory, there are some general points of agreement about the impact of globalization and global governance on the prospects of democracy. First, in addition to the widespread rejection of world government, there is general agreement about the limits of liberal representative democracy located within the nation-state under conditions of globalization. While cosmopolitan democracy gives the most direct and detailed account of the eroding capacities of citizens to exercise public rule through the state, deliberative approaches also emphasize the failure of the state to create inclusive forms of dialogue and deliberation that can meaningfully address global problems. Indeed, even liberal internationalists who are comfortable locating democracy within the nation-state contend that global governance arrangements need to develop enhanced forms of accountability to ensure they do not extinguish national democracy. Likewise, social democrats ground their normative claims in a reformist or revolutionary role for democratic states, but also put considerable emphasis on the role of international workers movements in regulating the global economy. More radically, Hardt and Negri argue that liberal democracy is oppressive because it is corrupted by state sovereignty and the imperatives of capitalism. The common theme here is that democracy must to some extent be extended beyond the nation-state in order realize or protect the democratic freedoms of citizens in an age of globalization.

Second, there is also a prominent theme in the literature that suggests democracy must not only be globalized, but also to some extent *socialized*. This is most clearly evident in the social democratic and radical approaches that seek to reform or overturn capitalism in order to create democratic communities that are responsive to human needs rather than financial markets. But it is also evident in the deliberative approach that argues for subjecting economic discourses and practices, such as those associated with neoliberalism, to widespread public deliberation that includes a wide range of social and environmental perspectives. Cosmopolitan approaches, and even the liberal approaches, contain advocates for socially oriented policies to ensure democratic rights and capabilities can be realized in a global context. Within the cosmopolitan democracy approach, for example, David Held argues for a catalogue of policies aimed at social justice and social solidarity to establish the conditions for effective participation and a fair and equal electoral system. While liberal internationalists are much more restrained in this regard, some scholars such as Daniel Deudney and John G. Ikenberry call for a return to the social underpinnings of liberal internationalism to restore the balance between capitalism and socioeconomic equity within the democratic world. This would enable an effective and *attractive* international community of democracies to counter the existing authoritarian states. What all these perspectives share is the idea that some attention must be paid to establishing social conditions that make democracy meaningful, effective and attractive to citizens all over the world.

Finally, there is also widespread agreement about the importance of civil society in creating more transparent and accountable global governance. Apart from the radical approach of Hardt and Negri, transparency and accountability figure prominently in the normative frameworks and programs for change in global democratic theory. Indeed, all approaches agree that technocratic effectiveness is not the only or best standard by which to judge global governance, nor is it any more important than democratic criteria and mechanisms of public oversight. In this regard, the inclusion of civil society actors is a central element of enhancing the transparency and accountability of global governance because they can play important roles in channelling up the knowledge and concerns of citizens, while also monitoring the activities of global governance for citizens that are distant or excluded from its decision-making processes. While the deliberative and radical approaches place central importance on civil

society or the multitude cooperating outside of state control, cosmopolitan democrats and social democrats also ground their arguments
in some form of transnational social activity. Furthermore, despite
its ambivalence to civil society, the liberal internationalist approach
does acknowledge the growing existence of transnational actors and
their contribution to pluralizing world politics, even though it sees
only minimal potential for it to enhance the accountability of global
governance.

These areas of agreement provide only a broad outline of the main
concerns of global democratic theory. Perhaps more significant in
terms of mapping the literature and developing concrete democratic
responses to globalization are the areas of disagreement. The global
democratic theory literature clearly contains wide differences not
only with regard to the central vision that each approach attempts to
realize, but also in relation to the kinds of institutions that could fea-
sibly be developed. These differences are reflected in various design
choices that are explained in the next section. While the argument of
cosmopolitan democracy and its advocacy of a global legal and electoral system in the 1990s was in many respects the origin of global
democratic theory, many scholars have since based their approach on
an explicit rejection of a global system of law and democracy, often
in direct critique of the cosmopolitan democracy scholarship. Liberal
internationalism and social democracy ground democracy primarily
in the nation-state without seeing the need for cosmopolitan democratic institutions, and transnational deliberative democracy and
radical democracy contend that the global architecture of cosmopolitan democracy is unfeasible, undesirable and unnecessary because
they seek a form of democracy that rests upon non-electoral avenues
of democratic practice.

These debates with cosmopolitan democracy reveal widespread
disagreement within global democratic theory concerning the desirable location of political community. Liberal internationalists and
social democrats still see political community as a primarily national
affair, while cosmopolitan democracy, deliberative democracy and
radical democracy see global and transnational political communities
emerging and thus democracy beyond the state as being both possible
and necessary. They also highlight another general point of difference
concerning the form of democracy itself. In many cases, scholars
are arguing for a form of democracy that is dramatically different
from liberal representative democracy and its focus on elections,
law and authorized representatives bound to a specific territory. For
example, transnational deliberative democracy, social democracy

and radical democracy explicitly seek to transcend liberal approaches and attempt to develop more inclusive forms of democratic practice that are broader ranging in scope and underpinned by social justice.

The value of global democratic theory lies in its articulation of a range of approaches that can help citizens to make sense of the changes underway as a result of globalization and critically rethink the democratic organization of national and global governance. The purpose of this book has been to present these approaches as a common body of theory in order to outline the diverse range of views, but also to encourage consideration of the approaches in relation to each other so that a productive dialogue can be established between them in order to advance scholarly debates and foster further refinement of the theories. More importantly, however, it is hoped that presenting the approaches in this way can be useful in informing practical action by citizens by allowing them to recognize common ground, consider the reasons for their different political choices, and crucially, widen political imaginations about how democracy might operate in the future to improve the organization of global governance.

Global Democratic Futures

Clearly, national and global governance have undergone significant changes due to the impact of globalization and neo-liberal reforms in recent decades. While it is the case that the liberalization and privatization agenda of neo-liberalism has restricted representative democracy in many ways, public pressure has also resulted in increasing forms of citizen engagement with governance apparatuses. Many global governance bodies like the WTO, World Bank and G20 have since the mid-1990s increased their public engagement and outreach to buttress their legitimacy (Esty 2002; O'Brien et al. 2000; Scholte 2011b). Furthermore, the recent development of transnational networks of governance in specific policy domains ranging from banking supervision to environmental compliance involve greater participation with key public stakeholders, even if there is less general oversight from elected representatives (Hale and Held 2011: 29). In many cases, NGOs and social movements have demanded access and succeeded in gaining participation in various fora of national and global policy-making. These trends have shifted decision-making authority away from governments that at least nominally represent societies as a whole, to technocrats and non-official actors with more specific interests and questionable representative credentials. This has led to renewed interest in the kinds of individuals, movements and organizations that will be the prime drivers of democratization along transnational or cosmopolitan lines (Archibugi and Held 2011; Archibugi, et al. 2012; Bray 2011; Scholte 2011b). The scholarship of global democratic theory contributes to our understanding of the problems and possibilities for democracy in this context. It provides the theoretical frameworks to analyze and support the democratic potential of these developments and thus contributes to efforts to rethink and redesign democracy on a global scale.

The capacity of global democratic theory to rethink democracy is evident in its wide-ranging ethical visions. In this regard, the first step in reconsidering the future of democracy is to destabilize the notion that elected representation within the nation-state is the only way to conceive of democratic life. Presenting electorally representative states as merely one interpretation of democracy among a range of alternatives opens up the political imaginary of citizens and widens the basis for democratic innovations. While there is little doubt that liberal representative democracy has fostered major positive advances in the development of public rule, global democratic theory scholarship also raises serious questions about its future given the impact of globalization and growing significance of global governance. Specifically, it contains profound criticisms of the existing liberal model and the way it privileges powerful domestic interests at the expense of others, particularly the interests of people living outside the nation-state who are nevertheless affected by the decisions made by those living within it. Concerns about excluded outsiders explains the prominence of the all-affected principle as a guide to extending democracy beyond the territory of any one state, either as a global constitutional principle defining political communities (cosmopolitan democracy), an ideal that frames deliberation across national borders (deliberative democracy), or a supplementary benchmark that shapes mechanisms of accountability within government networks (liberal internationalism). Furthermore, concerns that policymaking in many liberal states is heavily influenced by wealthy citizens and the interests of capitalists has led to alternative deliberative, social democratic and radical visions of political economy which include democratizing the global economy. This kind of thinking provides a stark contrast to dominant conceptions of democracy linked to political liberalism and a capitalist economy. As such, global democratic theory as a whole seeks to defend the democratic freedoms of citizens by avoiding oligarchy and world government, but also provides alternatives to the dominant liberal approaches to these issues.

In addition to opening up democratic futures, global democratic theory also provides specific political alternatives that reflect a number of key design choices. The first major design choice relates to the *institutionalization of democracy*. A major fault line in global democratic theory exists between "top-down" constitutional perspectives on democracy, which advocate the creation of formal democratic structures with electoral and judicial components, and "bottom-up" discursive perspectives on democracy, which advocate the cultivation of public cooperation and deliberation in a common "lifeworld" detached from formal institutions in national or transnational settings. Constitutional perspectives are evident in the approaches of liberal internationalism, cosmopolitan democracy and social democracy, while discursive approaches are articulated within deliberative and radical democracy. However, while the emphasis is usually placed on one or the other, most scholars do not exclusively focus on either constitutional design or generating informal publics. For example, some scholars in the deliberative democracy tradition explore ways to formally institutionalize deliberative theory (Dryzek and Niemeyer 2008), or base the solidarity of democratic publics on "constitutional patriotism" (Habermas 1999). More broadly, in order to ensure deliberation has a consequential effect on formal decision-making, deliberative democrats need to consider how to change existing constitutional rules that privilege the aggregation of votes. Conversely, constitutional accounts such as cosmopolitan democracy rely upon communication and deliberation in civil society to inform representative processes and must consider the social and cultural conditions required for the ongoing support of constitutional rules. Generally speaking, the question of whether democracy requires formal constitutionalism looms as an important question in establishing the nature and feasibility of democracy beyond the nation-state.

Another contentious issue concerning institutionalization is the role of the state in democratic politics (see also Chapter 1). While the approaches of cosmopolitan, transnational deliberative and radical democratic theory wish to downgrade or abolish the connection between democracy and the state, liberal internationalism, social democracy and republican elements of deliberative theory place considerable importance on the state's role in institutionalizing democratic politics. Deliberative and radical accounts of global democratic theory are evident in the activity of protest movements like the Occupy Movement, which point to the participatory political spaces that can be created offering variegated forms of politics that stand in opposition to prevailing patterns of dominance and power. However, most scholars in global democratic theory recognize that the state will continue to be an important component of governance, despite the rising importance of global governance and transnational civil society. This means that how each of the approaches reconciles their account of democracy to the ongoing presence of the state remains an important ongoing question. At worst, states can act to significantly undermine transnational forms of activism and democracy. Even in a more positive sense, there are still important questions to be answered about how transnational forms of activism and democratic practice can productively interface with the state and citizens. As such, the work of deliberative and republican theory concerning the dual role of citizens acting politically within their state and within transnational civil society appears to be an important line of inquiry. It is important because the global constitutionalism of cosmopolitan democracy appears to be an unlikely prospect in the near future and state constitutionalism alone is insufficient to deal with the growing number of global problems. In order to develop a substantial account of how to respond to globalization, more consideration needs to be given to how people can act as democratic citizens in both domestic and transnational contexts in the absence of a densely constitutionalized global system.

A second key design choice refers to the *scope of public issues subject to democratic control*. Clearly, liberal democrats are comfortable with a limited account of democratic scope to avoid the tyranny of the majority and preserve natural freedoms by creating an inviolable private sphere outside of political control. These limits are clearly demonstrated in the governance of economic issues where there is a strong commitment to recognizing the importance of private property rights and delegating decision-making processes to markets, technocratic officials, and central bankers. The contemporary strength of these limits is demonstrated by the compromised efforts of the Third Way to depart from neo-liberal orthodoxy. Most positions in global democratic theory contest the neo-liberal "hands off" approach to the global economy, but vary in the extent to which they want to regulate capitalism in order to realize democracy. While liberal internationalists and cosmopolitans wish to retain capitalism, to varying degrees they argue that enhancing the governance of global markets is necessary to provide public goods and stabilize economic activity. The other approaches argue for much greater democratic control. Social democratic, deliberative and radical accounts develop broader accounts of the scope of democracy, especially with regards to how democratic activity should inform economic policy-making. These approaches have accounts of democracy that make economic issues a central facet of public deliberation and determination, rather than leaving economic decisions to technocrats and markets that are insulated from democracy. Again, scholars within these approaches differ with regard to how far democracy should control economic life. Some social democrats want to reform capitalism and redistribute resources, while other social and radical democrats and express vehement opposition to capitalism and wish to see democratic planning of economic activity in order to realize equality. The recent crises in global capitalism have generated renewed debates over the level of public control over economic policy-making and this has renewed interest in social democratic, participatory and radical traditions of thought, as evident in the recent development of protest movements in the US and Europe (Isakhan and Slaughter 2014; Scholte 2011b, 2014).

A third key design choice relates to the *scale and nature of political community*. In terms of scale, while liberalism accepts human rights as a universal principle, these rights tend to be interpreted as moral values that need to be embedded in national politics, rather than as political ideals involving questions of citizenship, loyalty and collective political agency that would grant political rights to outsiders. As such, liberal internationalists do not conceive of a political community of citizens beyond the nation-state. All of the other approaches of global democratic theory, in contrast, do have an account of political community that exists beyond or across national boundaries, whether this is based on the all-affected principle, existing channels of communication, or immaterial production. However, these various accounts of political community envision different possibilities concerning the relationship between the individual and the collective, as well as different ways of dealing with questions of difference and internal dissent. Deliberative, social democratic and radical approaches conceive of communities based on consensus among citizens and have a high tolerance for dissent, but it must also be noted that social democracy assumes a community committed to moderating capitalism, and deliberative and radical accounts assume meta-agreement among citizens about the value of inclusion and wide-ranging participation in common activities. While further research is certainly needed to examine to what extent these political visions are emerging in contemporary social movements, the key issue is that the nature of political community and questions of identity and political loyalty are being challenged by globalization. Global democratic theory offers differing accounts of how existing forms of political community could be transformed from prevailing conceptions of nationalism.

Underlying these design choices is the issue of how citizens ought to use the approaches of global democratic theory. While many proposals have the character of plans or institutional blueprints, it is also important to see them as approaches that can be applied more pragmatically and selectively. Some approaches, such as cosmopolitan democracy, are fairly complete in their vision, but other approaches could be applied in part and selectively combined with others. For example, liberal internationalist proposals for enhancing the accountability and transparency of global governance could be combined with elements of deliberative and social democracy directed at improving the deliberative and representative credentials of its institutions, particularly in economic areas. Outside of formal institutions of the state, there are examples of practical social democratic efforts to develop collectives and other forms of democratic wealth ownership (Guinan 2013), and other forms of grass roots participation underpinned by deliberative and radical theories of democracy. Indeed, there are signs that we are entering a new phase of public participation in global governance, but this phase has the character of incremental and piecemeal democratizing shifts rather than wholesale changes in global governance. This suggests that a pragmatic approach to global democratic theory is warranted that avoids purely top-down approaches centred on elite-led constitutional change prominent in liberal internationalist and cosmopolitan theories, or purely bottom-up approaches centred on the deliberative and oppositional capacities of civil society and social movements prominent in the deliberative and radical approaches. This pragmatic approach suggests that the best prospects for global or transnational democracy emerge when broad coalitions involving states, international organizations and NGOs use their combined political and moral power to democratize a specifically problematic issue or institution. As such, the approaches covered in this book can help to identify common ground that could develop mutually beneficial coalitions. Further engagement and dialogue between the approaches would help to refine arguments and proposals that could be used on the ground. In helping to build these coalitions, the approaches analyzed in this book can be important reference points and serve as practical guidelines for citizens and leaders to create a more democratic world.

Conclusion

This book has argued that global democratic theory is a field of scholarship that examines democracy in an age of globalization and consequently makes an important contribution to understanding and guiding democratic politics in a complex and challenging global context. In an era where democracy is more widespread but also more constrained by the displacement of decision-making to global governance and global markets, it is important to think critically about the future of liberal democracy located within the nation-state and widen our political imaginations to include alternative forms of democratic practice and new ways of designing democracy. From this angle, it is also important to consider the limits and future of global democratic theory itself. Clearly, other areas of scholarship such as the global governance and global political economy literature are important complements to global democratic theory in understanding the changes underway in the contemporary world. While global democratic theory focuses upon the disjuncture between the state-based democracy and the globalization of politics, other disciplines also offer crucial insights into the changing context of global politics. Moreover, it is necessary to point out that global democratic theory originated as a predominantly Western discourse, which will increasingly have to engage with non-Western political theories and political practice in the future as the fates of communities all over the world become more globally intertwined.

Finally, it is important to reflect on the untenable nature of our current circumstances. Despite the globalization of economic, social, political, and cultural relations, and despite the fact that democracy has become the main legitimating principle of political rule, democracy is still confined to the domestic spheres of some nation-states. In this context, there are important questions to be answered about how people can meaningfully participate in the full range of governance institutions that shape their daily lives. In recent decades, the shortcomings of national democracy in dealing with global problems such as climate change and financial crises, as well as recognition of the "democratic deficits" of existing global governance, have generated a range of social movements and forms of activism that seek to shape the agenda of global decision-making and attempt to express public views that go beyond state interests. As such, it is important to remember that we are at the "beginning" of considering transnational democracy rather than at the end (Goodin 2010) and the reflections of democratic theory can assist leaders and citizens in understanding the impact of globalization on democracy and the problems and possibilities of new forms of democratic politics on a global scale. Global democratic theory can contribute to developing the political knowledge required by citizens to respond to the impact of globalization on the democratic state as well as help them to identify the democratic opportunities in global governance and transnational civil society. Global democratic theory thus offers a wide array of insights concerning how to rethink and redesign democracy in an increasingly globalized world.

Key Readings

Archibugi, D. and Held, D. (2011) Cosmopolitan democracy: paths and agents. *Ethics and International Affairs*, 25 (4), 433–61.

Archibugi, D., Koenig-Archibugi, M. and Marchetti, R. (2012) *Global Democracy: Normative and Empirical Perspectives.* Cambridge University Press, Cambridge.

Goodin, R. (2010) Global democracy: in the beginning. *International Theory* 2 (2), 175–209.

Scholte, J. A. (2014) Reinventing global democracy. *European Journal of International Relations*, 20 (1), 3–28.

Scholte J. A. (ed.) (2011) *Building Global Democracy? Civil Society and Accountable Global Governance.* Cambridge: Cambridge University Press.

References

#Occupy London (2013) *The Consensus Process*. http://occupylsx. org/?page_id=1999.

#OccupyTogether (2013) *Learn about #Occupy: background and timeline*. http://www.occupytogether.org/aboutoccupy/.

Agne, H. (2006) A dogma of democratic theory and globalization: why politics need not include everyone it affects. *European Journal of International Relations*, 12 (3), 433–458.

Anderson, B. (1991) *Imagined Communities*, revised edn. Verso, London and New York.

Annan, K. (2005) In larger freedom: towards development, security and human rights for all – executive summary. http://www.un.org/largerfree dom/summary.html.

Archibugi, D. (1998) Principles of cosmopolitan democracy. In Archibugi, D., Held, D., and Köhler, M. (eds.) *Re-Imagining Political Community: Studies in Cosmopolitan Democracy*. Polity, Cambridge, pp. 198–230.

Archibugi, D. (2004) Cosmopolitan democracy and its critics: a review. *European Journal of International Relations*, 10 (3), 437–73.

Archibugi, D. (2008) *The Global Commonwealth of Citizens: Toward Cosmopolitan Democracy*. Princeton University Press, Princeton and Oxford.

Archibugi, D. and Held, D. (2011) Cosmopolitan democracy: paths and agents. *Ethics and International Affairs*, 25 (4), 433–61.

Archibugi, D., Balduni, S. and Donati, M. (2000) The United Nations as an agency of global democracy. In Holden, B. (ed.) *Global Democracy: Key Debates*. Routledge: London and New York, pp. 125–42.

Archibugi, D., Koenig-Archibugi, M. and Marchetti, R. (2012) *Global Democracy: Normative and Empirical Perspectives*. Cambridge University Press, Cambridge.

Barber, B. (1984) *Strong Democracy: Participatory Politics for a New Age*. University of California Press, Berkeley and Los Angeles.

Barber, B. (1998) Democracy at risk: American culture in a global culture. *World Policy Journal*, 15 (2), 29–41.

Barnett M. and Duvall R. (2005), Power in global governance. In Barnett M. and Duvall R. (eds.), *Power in Global Governance* (Cambridge University Press, Cambridge).

Bellamy, R. and Barry Jones, R. J. (2000) Globalization and democracy – an afterword. In Holden, B. (ed.) *Global Democracy: Key Debates*. Routledge, London and New York, 202–16.

Benhabib, S. (2009) Cosmopolitanism and democracy: affinities and tensions. *The Hedgehog Review*, 11 (3), 30–41.

Blair, T. (1999) The Blair Doctrine: speech by the UK Prime Minister April 22, 1999. http://www.pbs.org/newshour/bb/international-jan-june99–blair_doctrine4–23/ .

Bob, C. (2002) Merchants of morality. *Foreign Policy* 129 (Mar/Apr), 36–45.

Bohman, J. (2007) *Democracy across Borders: From Dêmos to Dêmoi*. MIT Press, Cambridge.

Bohman, J. (2008) Transnational democracy and nondomination. In Laborde, C. and Maynor, J. (eds.) *Republicanism and Political Theory*. Blackwell, London, pp. 190–218.

Bohman, J. (2010) Introducing democracy across borders. *Ethics and Global Politics* 3, 1–11.

Brassett, J. and Smith, W. (2008) Deliberation and global governance: liberal, cosmopolitan and critical perspectives. *Ethics and International Affairs*, 22 (1), 69–92.

Brassett, J. and Smith, W. (2010) Deliberation and global civil society: Agency, arena, affect. *Review of International Studies*, 36 (2), 413–30.

Bray, D. (2011) *Pragmatic Cosmopolitanism: Representation and Leadership in Transnational Democracy*. Palgrave Macmillan, Basingstoke.

Bray, D. (2014) Neoliberal governance and the protest politics of the Occupy movement. In Isakhan, B. and Slaughter, S. (eds.) *Democracy and Crisis: Democratising Governance in the Twenty-First Century*. Basingstoke: Palgrave Macmillan, pp. 88–107.

Brown, G. (2011) Bringing the state back into cosmopolitanism: the idea of responsible cosmopolitan states. *Political Studies Review* 9, 53–66.

Browne, C. (2006) Democratic paradigms and the horizons of democratization. *Contretemps* 6, 43–58.

Buchanan, A. (2000) Rawls's law of peoples: rules for a vanished Westphalian world. *Ethics*, 110 (4), 697–721.

Buchanan, A. and Keohane, R. O. (2006) The legitimacy of global governance institutions. *Ethics and International Affairs*, 20 (4), 405–37.

Bull, H. (1995 [1977]) *The Anarchical Society. A Study of Order in World Politics*, 2nd edn. Macmillan, London.

Byrne, J. (ed.) (2012) *The Occupy Handbook*. Little, Brown, New York.

Callinicos, A. (2001) *Against the Third Way*. Polity, Cambridge.

Callinicos, A. (2003) *An Anti-Capitalist Manifesto*. Polity, Cambridge.

Callinicos, A. (2010) Commonwealth (Book Review). http://www.socialis-treview.org.uk/article.php?articlenumber=11189.

Carnoy, M. and Castells, M. (2001) Globalization, the knowledge society, and the network state: Poulantzas at the millennium. *Global Networks* 1 (1), 1–18.

Carr, E. H. (1946) *The Twenty Years' Crisis, 1919–1939*. Perennial, New York.

Castells, M. (1997) *The Power of Identity*, Vol. II of *The Information Age: Economy, Society and Culture*. Blackwell, Oxford.

Castells, M. (2008) The new public sphere: global civil society, communication networks, and global governance. *The ANNALS of the American Academy of Political and Social Science* 616 (1), 78–93.

Castells, M., Caraca, J., and Cardoso, G. (2012) The cultures of the economic crisis: an introduction. In Castells, M., Caraca, J., and Cardoso, G. (eds.) *Aftermath: The Cultures of the Economic Crisis*. Oxford University Press, Oxford, pp. 1–16.

Cerny, P. (1995) Globalisation and the changing nature of collective action. *International Organisation* 49 (4), 595–625.

Cerny, P. (1996) What next for the state? In Kofman, E. and Youngs, G. (eds.) *Globalisation: Theory and Practice*. Pinter, London, pp. 123–37.

Cerny, P. (1997) Paradoxes of the competition state: the dynamics of political globalisation. *Government and Opposition* 32 (2), 251–274.

Cerny, P. (1999) Globalisation and the erosion of democracy. *European Journal of Political Research* 36 (1), 1–26.

Cerny, P. (2000) Restructuring the political arena: globalisation and the paradoxes of the competition state. In Germain, R. D. (ed.) *Globalization and Its Critics: Perspectives from Political Economy*. Macmillan, London, pp. 117–38.

Cerny, P. (2009) The competition state today. *Policy Studies* 31 (1), 5–21.

Chambers, S. and Kopstein, J. (2001) Bad civil society. *Political Theory*, 29 (6), 837–65.

Chandler, D. (2003) New rights for old? Cosmopolitan citizenship and the critique of state sovereignty. *Political Studies* 51, 332–49.

Chomsky, N. (2002) *Understanding Power: The Indispensable Chomsky*. New Press, New York.

Clark, I. (2003) Legitimacy in a global order. *Review of International Studies*, 29, 75–95.

Clark, I. (2005) *Legitimacy in International Society*. Oxford University Press, Oxford.

Claude, I. (1971) *Swords into Ploughshares*. Random House, New York.

Clinton, B. (1996) *Between Hope and History*. Random House, New York.

Cole, G. D. H. (1920) *Social Theory*. Methuen, London.

Commission on Global Governance (1995) *Our Global Neighbourhood*. Oxford University Press, Oxford.

Cox, R. W. (1996) *Approaches to World Order*. Cambridge University Press, Cambridge.

Crouch, C. (2004) *Post-Democracy*. Polity, Cambridge.

Crouch, C. (2013) *Making Capitalism Fit for Society*. Polity, Cambridge.

Dagger, R. (2006) Neo-republicanism and the civic economy. *Politics, Philosophy and Economics* 5 (2): 151 –73.

Dahl, R. A. (1999) Can international organizations be democratic? A skeptic's view. In Shapiro, I. and Hacker-Cordón, C. (eds.) *Democracy's Edges*. Cambridge, Cambridge University Press, pp. 19–36.

Deudney, D. and Ikenberry, G. J. (2012) *Democratic Internationalism: An American Grand Strategy for a Post-Exceptionalist Era*. Council of Foreign Relations, New York. http://www.cfr.org/grand-strategy/demo cratic-internationalism-american-grand-strategy-post-exceptionalist-era/ p29417.

Doyle, M. W. (1986). Liberalism and world politics. *American Political Science Review* 80 (4), 1151–69.

Dryzek, J. (1999) Transnational democracy. *Journal of Political Philosophy* 7 (1), 30–51.

Dryzek, J. (2001) Legitimacy and economy in deliberative democracy. *Political Theory* 29 (5), 651–69.

Dryzek, J. (2004) Democratic political theory. In Gaus, G. and Kukathas, C. (eds.) *The Handbook of Political Theory*. Sage, London, pp. 143–54.

Dryzek, J. (2006) *Deliberative Global Politics: Discourse and Democracy in a Divided World*. Polity, Cambridge

Dryzek, J. (2010) *Foundations and Frontiers of Deliberative Governance*. Oxford University Press, Oxford.

Dryzek, J. (2011) Global democratization: Soup, society, or system? *Ethics and International Affairs*, 25 (2), 211–34.

Dryzek, J. (2012) Global civil society: the progress of post-Westphalian politics. *Annual Review of Political Science* 15, 101–19.

Dryzek, J. and Niemeyer, S. (2008) Discursive representation. *American Political Science Review* 102 (4), 481–93.

Dryzek, J., Bachtiger, A., and Milewicz, K. (2011) Toward a deliberative Global Citizens' Assembly. *Global Policy* 2 (1), 33–42.

Eckersley R. (2004) *The Green State: Rethinking Democracy and Sovereignty*. MIT Press, Cambridge, MA.

Eckersley, R. (2011) Representing Nature. In Alonso, S., Keane, J. and Merkel, W. (eds.) *The Future of Representative Democracy*. Cambridge University Press: Cambridge, pp. 236–57.

Esty, D. (2002) The World Trade Organisation's legitimacy crisis. *World Trade Review* 1(1), 7–22.

Falk, R. (1995) *On Humane Governance: Toward a New Global Politics*. Polity, Cambridge.

Falk, R. (1997) Resisting "globalisation-from-above" through "globalisa-tion-from-below." *New Political Economy* 2 (1), 17–24.

Falk, R. and Strauss, A. (2000) On the creation of a Global Peoples Assembly: legitimacy and the power of popular sovereignty. *Stanford Journal of International Law* 36, 191–220.

Falk, R. and Strauss, A. (2001) Toward global parliament. *Foreign Affairs* 80 (1), 212–20.

Foucault, M. (2004) *"Society Must Be Defended": Lectures at the Collège de France, 1975–76*. Penguin, London.

Foust, C. (2010) *Transgression as a Mode of Resistance: Rethinking Social Movement in an Era of Corporate Globalization*. Plymouth, Lexington Books.

Freedom House (1999) Democracy's century: a century of global political change in the 20th century. http://www.social-sciences-and-humanities. com/PDF/century_democracy.pdf.

Galtung, J. (2000) Alternative models for democracy. In Holden, B. (ed.) *Global Democracy: Key Debates*. Routledge, London and New York, pp. 143–61.

Gamble, A. (2009) Moving beyond the national: the challenges for social democracy in a global world. In Cramme, O. and Diamond, P. (eds.) *Social Justice in the Global Age*, Polity, Cambridge, pp. 117–35.

Gamble, A. (2010) The future of social democracy, *Social Europe Journal*. http://www.social-europe.eu/2010/01/the-future-of-social-democracy-2/.

Gellner, E. (1983). *Nations and Nationalism*. Blackwell, Oxford.

Germain, R. (2010) Financial governance and transnational deliberative democracy. *Review of International Studies* 36 (2), 493–509.

Giddens, A. (1985) *A Contemporary Critique of Historical Materialism*, Vol. 2: *The Nation State and Violence*. Polity, Cambridge.

Giddens, A. (1998) *The Third Way*. Polity, Cambridge.

Giddens, A. (2000) *The Third Way and Its Critics*. Polity, Cambridge.

Gill, S. (1995) Globalisation, market civilisation, and disciplinary neoliberalism. *Millennium* 24 (3), 399–423.

Gill, S. (1998) New constitutionalism, democratisation and global political economy. *Global Change, Peace and Security* 10 (1), 23–38.

Gill, S. (2012) Introduction: Global crises and the crisis of global leadership. In Gill, S. (ed.) *Global Crises and the Crisis of Global Leadership*. Cambridge University Press, Cambridge, pp. 1–19.

Gitlin, T. (2011) The left declares its independence. *New York Times*, 8 October. http://www.nytimes.com/2011/10/09/opinion/sunday/occupy-wall-street-and-the-tea-party.html?pagewanted=alland_r=0.

Glenn, H. P. (2013) *The Cosmopolitan State*. Oxford University Press, Oxford.

Goodin, R. (2010) Global democracy: in the beginning. *International Theory* 2 (2), 175–209.

Goodin, R. (2012) How can deliberative democracy get a grip? *The Political Quarterly* 83 (4), 806–11.

Goodin, R. and Ratner, S. R. (2011) Democratizing international law. *Global Policy* 2 (3), 241–7.

Gould, C. (2004) *Globalizing Democracy and Human Rights*. Cambridge University Press, Cambridge and New York.

Gould, C. (2006) Self-determination beyond sovereignty: relating transnational democracy to local autonomy. *Journal of Social Philosophy* 37 (1), 44–60.

Grant, R. and Keohane, R. O. (2005) Accountability and abuses of power in world politics. *American Political Science Review* 99 (1), 29–43.

Guinan, J. (2013) Social democracy in the age of austerity: the radical potential of democratizing capital. *Renewal* 20 (4), 9–19.

Haas, P. M. (1992) Introduction: epistemic communities and international policy coordination. *International Organization* 46 (1), 1–35.

Habermas, J. (1996) *Between Facts and Norms: Contributions to a Discourse Theory of Law and Democracy*. The MIT Press, Cambridge, MA.

Habermas, J. (1998) Three normative models of democracy. In Cronin, C. and De Greiff, P. (eds.) *The Inclusion of the Other: Studies in Political Theory*. The MIT Press, Cambridge, MA, pp. 239–52.

Habermas, J. (1999) The European nation-state: on the past and future of sovereignty and citizenship. In Cronin, C. and De Greiff, P. (eds.) *The Inclusion of the Other: Studies in Political Theory*. Polity, Cambridge, pp. 105–27.

Habermas, J. (2001) *The Postnational Constellation*. Polity, Cambridge.

Hale, T and Held, D. (2011) *Handbook of Transnational Governance Innovation*. Polity, Cambridge.

Hale, T. and Held, D. (2012) Gridlock and innovation in global governance: the partial transnational solution, *Global Policy* 3 (2), 169–81.

Hale, T., Held, D. and Young, K. (2013) *Gridlock: Why Global Cooperation Is Failing when We Need It Most*. Polity, Cambridge.

Hardt, M. and Negri, A. (2000) *Empire*. Harvard University Press, Cambridge, MA and New York.

Hardt, M. and Negri, A. (2004) *Multitude: War and Democracy in the Age of Empire*. The Penguin Press, New York.

Hardt, M. and Negri, A. (2009) *Commonwealth*. Belknap Press, Cambridge, MA.

Hardt, M. and Negri, A. (2011) The fight for real democracy at the heart of Occupy Wall St. *Foreign Affairs*, 11 October. http://www.foreignaffairs. com/articles/136399/michael-hardt-and-antonio-negri/the-fight-for-real-democracy-at-the-heart-of-occupy-wall-street.

Hardt, M. and Negri, A. (2012) *Declaration*. Argo-Nevis, New York.

Harvey, D. (1997) *Justice, Nature and the Geography of Difference*. Basil Blackwell, Oxford.

Harvey, D. (2005) *A Brief History of Neoliberalism*. Oxford University Press, Oxford.

Harvey, D., Hardt, M. and Negri, A. (2009) Commonwealth: an exchange. *Artforum International* 48 (3): 210–21.

Hawthorn, G. (2003) Running the world through Windows. In Archibugi, D. (ed.) *Debating Cosmopolitics*. Verso, London, pp. 16–26.

Held, D. (1995) *Democracy and the Global Order: From the Modern State to Cosmopolitan Global Governance*. Stanford University Press, Stanford.

Held, D. (1998) Democracy and globalization. In Archibugi, D., Held, D., and Köhler, M. (eds.) *Re-imagining Political Community: Studies in Cosmopolitan Democracy*. Polity, Cambridge, pp. 11–27.

Held, D. (2000) The changing contours of political community: rethinking democracy in the context of globalization. In Holden, B. (ed.) *Global Democracy: Key Debates*. Routledge, London and New York, pp. 17–31.

Held, D. (2002) Law of states, law of peoples: three models of sovereignty. *Legal Theory* 8, 1–44.

Held, D. (2003) Cosmopolitanism: globalisation tamed? *Review of International Studies* 29, 465–480.

Held, D. (2004) *Global Covenant: The Social Democratic Alternative to the Washington Consensus*. Polity, Cambridge.

Held, D. (2006a) *Models of Democracy*, 3rd edn. Stanford University Press, Stanford.

Held, D. (2006b) Reforming global governance: apocalypse soon or reform! *New Political Economy* 11 (2), 157–76.

Held, D. (2010) *Cosmopolitanism: Ideas and Realities*. Polity, Cambridge.

Held, D., McGrew, A., Goldblatt, D., and Perraton, J. (1999) *Global Transformations: Politics, Economics and Culture*. Polity, Cambridge.

Held, D. and McGrew, A. (eds.) (2002) *Governing Globalization: Power, Authority and Global Governance*. Polity, Cambridge.

Held, D. and McGrew, A. (2007) *Globalization/Anti-Globalization: Beyond the Great Divide*, 2nd edn. Polity, Cambridge.

Higgott, R. and Erman, E. (2010) Deliberative global governance and the question of legitimacy: what can we learn from the WTO? *Review of International Studies* 36 (2), 449–70.

Hirst, P., Thompson, G. and Bromley, S. (2009) *Globalization in Question*, 3rd edn. Polity, Cambridge.

Holden, B. (ed.) (2000) *Global Democracy: Key Debates*. Routledge, London.

Huntington, S. (1991) *The Third Wave: Democratization in the Late Twentieth Century*. University of Oklahoma Press, Norman.

Hutton, W. (1996) *The State We're In*. Vintage, London.

Hutton, W. (1997) *The State to Come*. Vintage, London.

Isakhan, B. and Slaughter, S. (2014) Introduction: crisis and representative democracy in the twenty-first century. In B. Isakhan and S. Slaughter (eds.) *Democracy and Crisis: Democratising Governance in the Twenty-First Century*. Houndsmills, Palgrave Press, pp. 1–22.

Jackson, R. (1990) Martin Wight, international theory and the good life. *Millennium* 19 (2), 261–72.

Jolly, R. et al. (2005) *The Power of UN Ideas: Lessons from the First 60 Years*. Bloomington, Indiana University Press.

Judt, T. (2009) What is living and what is dead in social democracy? *New York Review of Books* Volume 56, Number 20, December 17. http://www.nybooks.com/articles/archives/2009/dec/17/what-is-living-and -what-is-dead-in-social-democrac/.

Juris, J. S. (2012) Reflections on #Occupy Everywhere: social media, public space, and emerging logics of aggregation. *American Ethnologist*, 39 (2), 259–79.

Keane, J. (2011) Monitory democracy. In Alonso, S., Keane, J., Merkel, W., and Fotou, M. (eds.) *The Future of Representative Democracy*. Cambridge University Press, Cambridge, pp. 212–35.

Keck, M. and Sikkink, K. (1998) *Activists Beyond Borders: Advocacy Networks in International Politics*. Cornell University Press, Cornell.

Keohane, R. O. (1984) *After Hegemony*. Princeton University Press, Princeton.

Keohane, R. O. (1998) International institutions: can interdependence work? *Foreign Policy*, 110, 82–96.

Keohane, R. O. (2001) Governance in a partially globalized world. *American Political Science Review* 95 (1), 1–13.

Keohane, R. O. (2003) Global governance and democratic accountability. In Held, D. and Koenig-Archibugi, M. (eds.) *Taming Globalization: Frontiers of Governance*. Polity, Cambridge, pp. 130–59.

Keohane, R. O. (2006) Accountability in world politics. *Scandinavian Political Studies*, 29 (2), 75–87.

Keohane, R. O. and Nye, J. S. (2001a) Between centralization and fragmentation: the club model of multilateral cooperation and problems of democratic legitimacy. John F. Kennedy School of Government Research Working Paper Series, Harvard University.

Keohane, R. O. and Nye, J. S. (2001b) *Power and Interdependence*, 3rd edn. Longman, New York.

Keohane, R. O., Macedo, S., and Moravcsik, A. (2009) Democracy-enhancing multilateralism. *International Organization* 63 (1), 1–31.

Kuper, A. (2004) *Democracy beyond Borders: Justice and Representation in Global Institutions*. Oxford University Press, Oxford.

Laborde, C. (2010) Republicanism and global justice: a sketch. *European Journal of Political Theory*, 9 (1), 48–69.

Lapavitsas, C (2014) *Profiting Without Producing: How Finance Exploits Us All*, Verso, London.

Lawson, N. (2011) Social democracy: in crisis the world over. http://www. opendemocracy.net/neal-lawson/social-democracy-in-crisis-world-over.

Linklater, A. (1998a) Citizenship and sovereignty in the post-Westphalian European state. In Archibugi, D., Held, D. and Köhler, M. (eds.) *Re-Imagining Political Community: Studies in Cosmopolitan Democracy*. Polity, Cambridge, pp. 113–37.

Linklater, A. (1998b) *The Transformation of Political Community*. University of South Carolina Press: Columbia.

MacDonald, T. (2008) *Global Stakeholder Democracy: Power and Representation Beyond Liberal States*. Oxford University Press, Oxford.

Macdonald, T. (2010) Corporations and global justice: rethinking "public" and "private" responsibilities. In Macdonald, K. and Marshall, S. (eds.) *Fair Trade, Corporate Accountability and Beyond: Experiments in Globalizing Justice*. Ashgate, Surrey, pp. 137–48.

Macdonald, T. and Ronzoni, M. (2012) Introduction: the idea of global political justice. *Critical Review of International Social and Political Philosophy* 15 (5), 521–33.

McGrew, A. (1997) Democracy beyond borders? Globalization and the reconstruction of democratic theory and practice. In McGrew, A. (ed.) *The Transformation of Democracy: Globalization and Territorial Democracy*. Polity, Cambridge, pp. 231–66.

McGrew, A. (2002a) Liberal internationalism: between realism and cosmopolitanism. In Held, D. and McGrew, A. (eds.) *Governing Globalization: Power, Authority and Global Governance*. Polity, Cambridge, pp. 267–89.

McGrew, A. (2002b) Transnational democracy: theories and prospects. In Stokes, G. and Carter, A. (eds.) *Democratic Theory Today: Challenges for the 21st Century*. Polity, Cambridge, pp. 269–94.

Marchetti, R. (2008) *Global Democracy: For and Against*. Routledge, London and New York.

Marquand, D. (1999) The *New Statesman* essay - The old Labour rocks re-emerge. *The New Statesman* 128 (4456), 43–6.

Martell, L. (2011) The future of cosmopolitan social democracy. http://www.academia.edu/990707/The_Future_for_Cosmopolitan_Social_Democracy.

Marx, K. and Engels, F. (1967 [1848]) *The Communist Manifesto*. Penguin, London.

Mingst, K. A. and Karns, M. (2007) *The United Nations in the 21st Century*, 3rd edn. Westview Press, Boulder.

Monbiot, G. (2003) *The Age of Consent: A Manifesto for a New World Order*. Harper Perennial, London.

Moravcsik, A. (2002) In defence of the "democratic deficit": reassessing legitimacy in the European Union. *Journal of Common Market Studies* 40 (4), 603–24.

Mouffe, C. (1999) Deliberative democracy or agonistic pluralism? *Social Research* 66 (3), 745–58.

Mouffe, C. (2000) *The Democratic Paradox*. Verso, London.

Mouffe, C. (2011) Democracy in a multipolar world. In Hoover, J., Sabaratnam, M. and Schouenborg, L. (eds.) *Interrogating Democracy in World Politics*. Routledge, London, pp. 118–29.

Muldoon, J. (ed.) (2012) *Occupy Reflects*. Melbourne. http://zinelibrary.info/files/Occupy%20Reflects.pdf.

Negri, A. (1999) *Insurgencies: Constituent Power and the Modern State*. University of Minneapolis Press, Minneapolis and London.

Nye, J. S. (2003) Introduction. In *The "Democracy Deficit" in the Global Economy: Enhancing the Legitimacy and Accountability of Global Institutions.* The Trilateral Commission, Washington, Paris, Tokyo, pp. 1–9.

O'Brien, R., Goetz, A. M., Scholte, J. A. and Williams, M. (2000) *Contesting Global Governance: Multilateral Economic Institutions and Global Social Movements.* Cambridge University Press, Cambridge.

Ohmae, K. (1995) Putting global logic first. *Harvard Business Review* 73 (1), 119–25.

Pateman, C. (1970) *Participation and Democratic Theory.* Cambridge University Press, Cambridge.

Pateman, C. (2012) Participatory democracy revisited. *Perspectives on Politics* 10 (1), 7–19.

Pettit, P. (1999a) *Republicanism.* Oxford University Press, Oxford.

Pettit, P. (1999b) Republican freedom and contestatory democratization. In Shapiro, I. and Hacker-Cordón, C. (eds.) *Democracy's Value.* Cambridge University Press, Cambridge, pp. 163–90.

Pettit, P. (2003) Deliberative democracy, the discursive dilemma, and republican theory. In Fishkin, J. and Laslett, P. (eds.) *Debating Deliberative Democracy.* Blackwell, Oxford, pp. 138–62.

Pettit, P. (2005) Two-dimensional democracy, national and international, IILJ Working Paper (History and Theory of International Law Series).

Pettit, P. (2010) Republican law of peoples. *European Journal of Political Theory* 9 (1), 70–94.

Pleyers, G. (2010) *Alter-Globalization: Becoming Actors in the Global Age.* Polity, Cambridge.

Pogge, T. (1992) Cosmopolitanism and sovereignty. *Ethics* 103 (1): 48–75.

Pogge, T. (2002) *World Poverty and Human Rights.* Polity: Cambridge.

Poggi, G. (1978) *The Development of the Modern State: A Sociological Introduction.* Stanford University Press, Stanford.

Rawls, J. (1999) *The Law of Peoples, with The Idea of Public Reason Revisited.* Harvard University Press, Cambridge, MA, and London.

Razsa, M. and Kurnik, A. (2012) The Occupy Movement in Žižek's hometown: direct democracy and politics of becoming. *American Ethnologist* 39 (2): 238–58.

Reich, R. (1991) *The Work of Nations.* London: Simon and Schuster.

Reus-Smit, C. (1998) Changing patterns of governance: from absolutism to global multilateralism. In Paolini, A., Jarvis, A. P., and Reus-Smit, C. (eds.). *Between Sovereignty and Global Governance: The United Nations, the State and Civil Society.* Macmillan, London, pp. 3–28.

Reus-Smit, C. (2007) International crises of legitimacy. *International Politics* 44 (2), 157–174.

Robbins, B. (2010) Multitude, are you there? (Book Review) *Self-Improvement* 10. http://nplusonemag.com/multitude-are-you-there.

Roberts, A. (2012) Why the Occupy movement failed. *Public Administration Review* 72 (5): 754–62.

Roper, B. (2011) Reformism on a global scale? A critical examination of David Held's advocacy of cosmopolitan social democracy. *Capital and Class*, 35, 253–73.

Rosenau, J.N. (1992) The relocation of authority in a shrinking world. *Comparative Politics* 24 (3), 253–72.

Rosenau, J. (1999) Toward an ontology for global governance. In Hewson, M. and Sinclair, T. J. (eds.) *Approaches to Global Governance Theory*. State University of New York, Albany, pp. 287–302.

Rupert, M. (1997) Globalization and the reconstruction of common sense in the US. In Gill, S. and Mittelman, J. (eds.) *Innovation and Transformation in International Studies*. Cambridge University Press, Cambridge, pp. 138–52.

Sassen, S. (2003) The state and globalization. *Interventions* 5 (2), 241–48.

Sassen, S. (2006) *Territory, Authority, Rights: From Medieval to Global Assemblages*. Princeton University Press, Princeton.

Saward, M. (2000) A critique of Held. In Holden, B. (ed.) *Global Democracy: Key Debates*. Routledge, London and New York, 32–46.

Saward, M. (2001) Reconstructing democracy: current thinking and new directions. *Government and Opposition* 36 (4), 559–81.

Saward, M. (2006) Democracy and citizenship: expanding domains. In Dryzek, J., Honig, B., and Phillips, A. (eds.) *The Oxford Handbook of Political Theory*. Oxford University Press, Oxford, pp. 400–22.

Scholte, J. A. (2000) *Globalisation, a Critical Introduction*. Palgrave, Basingstoke.

Scholte, J. A. (2002) Civil society and democracy in global governance. *Global Governance*, 8 (3), 281–304.

Scholte, J. A. (2011a) Towards greater legitimacy in global governance. *Review of International Political Economy* 18 (1), 110–20.

Scholte J. A. (ed.) (2011b) *Building Global Democracy? Civil Society and Accountable Global Governance*. Cambridge: Cambridge University Press.

Scholte, J. A. (2014) Reinventing global democracy. *European Journal of International Relations*, 20 (1), 3–28.

Shapiro, M. (2001) Administrative law unbounded: reflection on government and governance. *Indiana Journal of Global Legal Studies* 8, 369–77.

Sklair, L. (1997) Social movements for global capitalism: the transnational capitalist class in action. *Review of International Political Economy* 4 (3), 514–38.

Slaughter, A. (2003) Global government networks, global information agencies, and disaggregated democracy. *Michigan Journal of International Law*, 24, 1041–75.

Slaughter, A. (2004) *A New World Order*. Princeton University Press, Princeton and London.

Slaughter, S. (2005) *Liberty Beyond Neo-liberalism: a Republican Critique of Liberal Governance in a Globalising Age*. Palgrave, Houndmills.

Slaughter, S. (2013) The prospects of deliberative global governance in the G20: legitimacy, accountability, and public contestation. *Review of International Studies* 39 (1), 71–90.

Smith, S (1992) The forty years' detour: The resurgence of normative theory in international relations. *Millennium – Journal of International Studies* 21, 489–506.

Socialist International (1989) Declaration of principles. http://www.social istinternational.org/viewArticle.cfm?ArticleID=31.

Sørenson, G. (2004) *The Transformation of the State: Beyond the Myth of Retreat*. Palgrave Macmillan, Basingstoke.

Steffek, J. (2003) The legitimation of international governance. *European Journal of International Relations* 9 (2), 249–75.

Steffek, J. (2010) Public accountability and the public sphere of international governance. *Ethics and International Affairs* 24 (1), 45–67.

Steger, M. B. (2009) *Globalization: A Very Short Introduction*. Oxford University Press, Oxford.

Stiglitz, J. (2002) *Globalization and Its Discontents*. W. W. Norton, New York.

Stiglitz, J. (2012) *The Price of Inequality: How Today's Divided Society Endangers Our Future*. W. W. Norton, New York.

Stokes, G. (2006) Critical theories of deliberative democracy and the problem of citizenship. In Leib, E. J. and He, B. (eds.) *Search for Deliberative Democracy in China*. Palgrave Macmillan, New York, pp. 53–73.

Stone, D. (2008) Global public policy, transnational policy communities and their networks. *Policy Studies Journal* 36 (10), 19–38.

Strange, S. (1996) *Retreat of the State*. Cambridge University Press, Cambridge.

Tannsjo, T. (2008) *Global Democracy: The Case for a World Government*. Edinburgh University Press, Edinburgh.

UNDP (2002) *Human Development Report 2002: Deepening Democracy in a Fragmented World*. Oxford University Press, New York and Oxford.

Vandenberg, A. (2007) Social movement unionism. In Hudson, W. and Slaughter, S. (eds.) *Globalisation and Citizenship: The Transnational Challenge*. Routledge, London, pp. 137–49.

Waltz, K. N. (1999) Globalization and governance. *PS: Political Science and Politics* 32 (4), 693–700.

Waltz, K. N. (2000) Globalization and American power. *The National Interest*, Spring 59: 46–56.

Walzer, M, (1995) The concept of civil society. In Walzer, M. (ed.) *Toward a Global Civil Society*. Berghahn Books, New York, pp. 7–29.

Weber, M. (2009) Understanding and analysing social movements and alternative globalization. In Hayden, P. (ed.), *The Ashgate Research Companion to Ethics and International Relations*. Ashgate, pp. 427–42.

Weiler, J. H. H. (1999) To be a European citizen: Eros and civilization. In *The Constitution of Europe: "Do the New Clothes Have An Emperor" and*

Other Essays on European Integration. Cambridge University Press, New York.

Weiss, L. (1998) *The Myth of the Powerless State.* Cornell University Press, Ithaca.

Whelan, F. G. (1983) Prologue: democratic theory and the boundary problem. In Pennock, J. R. and Chapman, J. W. (eds.) *Liberal Democracy.* New York University Press, New York and London, pp. 13–47.

Wight, M. (1966) Why is there no international theory? In Butterfield, H., and Wight, M. (eds.), *Diplomatic Investigations: Essay in the Theory of International Politics.* Allen and Unwin, London, pp. 17–34.

Wilson, W. (1917) Joint address to Congress leading to a declaration of war against Germany. http://www.ourdocuments.gov/doc.php?doc=61.

Zolo, D. (1997) *Cosmopolis: Prospect for World Government.* Polity, Cambridge.

Index